RELENTLESS LIFE THROUGH BUMPS

OVERCOMING HURDLES IN LIFE

This book is book 2 in a series of 3 of Githii's autobiographical books.

An Autobiography of

DR. DAVID M. GITHII

DR. DAVID M. GITHII

Relentless Life Bumps

Published by KENCRIC CONSULTANTS
P. O. Box 4272-00200, Nairobi-Kenya.
Email: kencric99@gmail.com

ISBN: 978-1-968966-72-0

Initial Editing & Design by Emily Mukomunene,
Secondary editing by Winstone Sharrad.
Email: emukomunene2077@gmail.com
Secondary editing: Winstone Sharrad
Email: sharradm@yahoo.co.uk
Cover Design & Layout: Winstone Sharrad
Cover Image Credits: Unsplash.com-Troy-Williams

CONTENTS

1. ST. PAUL'S UNITED THEOLOGICAL COLLEGE 15

Ministry At Thogoto Parish 24
Neglected 28
The Origin Of Elder Districts In PCEA Church 35
Delayed Ordination 41
Ministry At Nakuru Parish 52
Elder District Competitions 57

2. DEDICATION OF PCEA RUGURU CHURCH 59

Pilgrim's Progress 62
Africanization Of The Church 65
Ministry At Rongai Parish 69

3. ESTABLISHMENT OF ELDER DISTRICTS AT RONGAI PARISH 80

Meeting All Elders 80
Engagements And Visitation 81
Fund-Raising 88
Pcea Pastoral Institute Students 92
Cohesiveness In Ministry 95
Ministry At Loresho Parish 100

4. OVERSEAS STUDIES 111

Picked From The Airport 111
Life At Dubuque University 118
The Struggle In Raising Money 125
Tom Kirkpatrick 127
The Funds Drive At Dr. Arthur Church 129
Dr. John Toay 133
The Photocopy 135

The Breakthrough 139
Two Days Stop Over In Atlanta 141
5. THE BEGINNING OF A MIRACULOUS PATH 144
The Flight From Atlanta To Fuller Seminary 144
The Connection With Dan And Cheryl 155
The Journey By Road To Fuller 157
Arrival At Fuller 164
Cultural Shock 166
The Visit By Tim And Thomsons 170
6. ENHANCED MIRACULOUS PATH 172
My Encounter With Flanagan-Miracle On Tuition 172
My Encounter With John 177
7. MONTE VISTA GROVE HOMES 182
Yet Another Miracle On Accomodation 182
The Breakthrough 189
Finally, A Residence At Monte Vista Grove Homes ... 196
8. TOUGH ACADEMIC TIMES 199
The Mysterious Side Path Walk 206
Divine Providence 219
Humiliation By A Professor 223
9. MINISTRY AT MUGUGA PARISH 227
Leadership Studies In Scotland 231
Senior Lecturer At Daystar Univesrisity 232

ACKNOWLEDGEMENT

In writing this book, I owe much gratitude to my wife, Lucy Wanjiku and my daughter, Terry Njoki, who bore an unquantifiable amount of sacrifice in kind and psychologically as I consumed the sunlight hours and withstanding long night hours with open eyes as I jotted what now is the "book". Many times, I denied them time and space and neither reciprocated their support. I was fully submerged in writing. In comradeship, they made sure that I was well-fed and that my needs were met accordingly. They ensured that the environment was conducive enough for my writing. Without their support, this book would not have been. I am also thankful to all my children: Benson Githii, Sammy Gicuki, Amos Thuku (Ndicu), Nicholas Githag'a and Mary Wangari. They kept patience and took interest, thus boosting the morale I required as I dug deep in the spirit and mind to bring out every aspect that ultimately formed the book. I'm grateful for all the support they have given me.

My gratitude to Tabitha James (Njeri) head of one of the programs at Kigocho Radio Station in Nairobi. She spent so much of her time and energy wrestling with the tedious work of writing my manuscript. She selflessly offered her services and even encouraged me the many times I felt like giving up as I got overwhelmed with research and writing. She was always urging me when I struggled to recall and clear events overlapping for many years in order to publish the correct information.

DEDICATION

This Book is dedicated to my wife and children.

Wife's name:
Lucy Wanjiku Muhia

Names of children:
Benson Githii, Sammy Gichuki, Amos Thuku, Nicholas Githang'a, Mary Wangari and Terry Njoki.

ABBREVIATIONS

GA	General Assembly.
GAC	General Administrate Committee.
PCEA	Presbyterian Church of East Africa.
PUEA	Presbyterian University of East Africa.

DISCLAIMER

In sharing my story, I recognize that navigating sensitive topics can sometimes lead to unintentional missteps. While the safest approach might be to avoid stepping forward entirely, my commitment to recounting my journey compels me to move forward, even if it means occasionally revisiting past experiences with the reader.

I extend my sincere apologies in advance to anyone who may find the contents of this publication distressing or offensive. Please understand that my intention is not to cause harm or to offend any individual or organization. I acknowledge that the pursuit of truth and the presentation of personal experiences can occasionally create friction with established norms or sensitivities.

Thank you for your understanding.

FOREWORD

I was introduced to David Githii by one of his enthusiastic friends after he coincidentally saw my publications. After reading the author's manuscripts, I knew that my encounter was not just a coincidence but one of God's many Divine connections in David's life. I remember the evening that I went to a computer and accessory shop to replace my laptop charger. In the shop, there was a gentleman with a small boy, maybe his son. I placed an order and he gave me the charger to test and confirm if it worked on my machine. In the process of removing my laptop, I placed some of my books on the counter. The back of the top book was facing upwards. So, as I fixed the charger to check if it was working, the gentleman was busy reading the brief on my cover book (blurb).

"You must be the author of this book. Who publishes your books?" He simultaneously asked me. I simply answered, *"Yes, I am, and we do have a publishing firm, too."* He quickly took his phone and jotted a number on a piece of paper as I paid for the charger. He gave me the piece of paper and told me that the contact was for someone who had a very good story that needed to be published. He requested me to call Dr. Githii, for he was looking for advice on publishing his story. I took the paper without much ado. Having gotten the charger, I safely packed my laptop and the books and left the shop.

The next day, as I unflapped my laptop, a piece of paper was stuck on the screen. It was the paper with Dr Githii's contact. I was quite busy and had no intention of calling him. A few days later, I came across the same paper on my table. It was then that I decided to give him a call and we got connected.

My encounter and involvement were not without opposition.

I remember at one time, I was in a car with some colleagues as we were heading to the All African Conference of Churches (AACC) office and I received a call from Dr. Githii. I answered his call with greetings, "*Good afternoon, Dr Githii...*" Our conversation was brief. When the call ended, I found my colleagues staring at me lugubriously, and they simultaneously asked me, "*Was that Githii the Moderator?*" I answered sure it was and that I was working on his book. I was shocked by the kind of talk they unleashed on me. To make matters short, one of them told me, "*Do not dare work with that man, for he will make your life complicated...*" Well, I had given him my word, and I'm one of those people who believe that "*A lady is not for turning*" unless otherwise, and when she turns, "*It is forward ever*" even in the turning. Anyway, one cannot hide a book, and publishing is teamwork. I lost a lot of my editing team when, as usual, I presented the manuscript for editing to them. When they rejected the work, I accepted it as their professional right to choose whom to work with as editors. In my view, the book "*Life Through The burning Bush*" brings out a rare quality of a man "*appointed*" by God. David reveals the honesty and naked truth that has eluded most leaders and belittled the faith of a people who would have otherwise been saved by the mercies of God. It portrays his life right after birth and the challenges he went through in very daring circumstances, especially during the colonial era in Kenya after his dad got detained for seven years because of leading the Mau Mau movement. It recounts how, by the grace of God, light shone for him at the apex of a hollow life in darkness. It talks about the time his dad was released from prison after many years of unquantifiable suffering, stigma and denial of very basic human rights such as food, accommodation and education.

Amusingly, at a certain phase of his life as a teacher, without recognizing that it was God who had preserved him, he embraced an alcoholic lifestyle, a story told in volume one of the series. It is *'a must read.'* God had to visit and rescue him from that reckless life because He had a mission for him. After this, God's Grace catapulted him, making a little-known person of a humble background to be known through his *"Excellent Leadership."* His abandonment of his career of choice and shunning *"a bright future"* as he responded to an invincible call that led him to join the Church Ministry is a manifestation of His faith in God. His story affirms that God uses the available. And in this case David is ready to embark on a journey of his life. It is not only, living *"Life Through the Burning Bush,"* but to even somersault through the burning bush *"Acts"* of his calling as the situation demands. This reminds me of the Biblical

David. It reminds me of the way he submerged his life to face Goliath, the bears and the lions.

The book delivers a potent true story of the author in an honest tone that super-changes your attitude towards God and life. It brings out a deep passion for obedience to God's voice that leads to deeper personal satisfaction. As you read it, you become part of the author's journey.

Winstone
Health Consultant/ Researcher, Author,
Publishing Editor & Social Entrepreneur

1. ST. PAUL'S UNITED THEOLOGICAL COLLEGE

I have explained my wretched early childhood life in my other book, "Life Through the Burning Bush" and whereby I have indicated "how I started my education at the age of 12. I have also talked about my academic success and how I embarked on teaching as my career of choice. I have also talked of my life as a headmaster of Cheptoroi Primary School as well as founder headmaster of Cheptoroi Secondary School. This is where, at the apex of my successful teaching career, as I awaited the appointment letter as an Area Education Officer (AEO), that I received a spiritual calling to join the Church Ministry. I abandoned a well-paying job and reported to St Paul's United Theological School in September of 1980. This is an ecumenical School under the umbrella of PCEA, Anglicans, Methodists and the Reformed Denomination, among others. It is located about 15 km South-East of Limuru Town.

Upon my arrival, the first person I met at the gate of the school introduced himself to me as Rev. Geoffrey Ngumi. I expected him to take hold of my box and lead the way to the reception desk of the school. This is exactly what happened after I had moved a few steps with my box. He helped me carry the box, and we checked for my name on the notice board. Ngumi then helped me to get to the reception to access the room allocated to me. He then opened the door of the room and left me there. This was either on a Monday or a Tuesday. The school started immediately. One of my classmates was Benson Kanina Kirikiru. We were both teaching at Cheptoroi Primary School. This is the very teacher who had forgotten to hand me my invitation letter to the Church interview. He had received the call slightly after I received mine. His way worked easily through the Anglican Church, where it seems most of the decisions are made by the bishop. Another of my former staff at Cheptoroi who joined St. Paul's Theological College a year later was Odongo. These two had come to accept Jesus as Lord and Saviour after I had preached to them, possibly not so much through verbal preaching but having watched my character and especially the love I had for God, the children, staff and parents. Thus, two former teachers of Cheptoroi Primary were now treading on the priesthood path with me. When Kirikiru married in our final year in college, my wife and I became their best couple. It was at St. Paul's that I first experienced the life of the Church. Here, there were students from many denominations. Each of these students from various denominations enriched one another as they interacted in classes, sports, chapel services, clubs, and Kamukunji (*a kind of common platform where students met at leisure to debate on different issues*). Such engagements extended to the library and in the dormitories. It was from all these people, and especially the Presbyterians, that I had to do all I could to learn more about the Church.

I very quickly made friends with other Presbyterian students, especially the eight we had done interviews with at the Pastoral Institute, who ended up joining the diploma class that had reported in January. It was from them that I had the first-hand information that the total number of candidates who had sat for the interview was sixty-four, and only nine had passed, of which I was number one. The eight had come on January 7th to undertake a diploma course. It was only me from the whole group who had qualified to undertake a degree course.

When I enquired about how many of us passed, Geoffrey Ngoima said,

"Surprisingly, the number of people who were interviewed were sixty-four and only nine passed and you happened to be number one."

I further inquired,

"And how did that happen yet I knew almost nothing about the PCEA constitution, it's by-laws and even the traditions?"

It is then Ngoima explained the fact that the area that carried over fifty percent of the total marks was the proof of one's call and the fact that I expressed myself quite well in my answer to the question, *"Tell us about yourself."*

He said that many of those interviewed had given very brief answers like, *"My name is John, a born again Christian, a church elder, married with two children..etc. But in your case, you gave very detailed aspects on your life. In addition, you led in the written examination."*

Another one, who called himself Gathairu, said,
> *"Yes, many of these candidates could write volumes about the Presbyterian Church of East Africa but they failed to satisfy the panel on the depth of their calling."*

Another person who was referred to as Gatua said,
> *"I hope you know you were number one overall, never forget that. This means that you topped the list of sixty-four candidates who had turned up for the interview including the eight of us who joined this college in January. You are the only one who then qualified for the Bachelor of Divininty degree hence, your coming here in September. We will do our best to help you settle down."*

That was a good revelation for me because I was not aware of it. I learnt from them that the call entails one's life and how one came to know and accept Christ's path of life, and also one's reasoning as to how he/she feels called by God. It also meant that one was not joining the Ministry because it was a way of getting a job, power or recognition, for *"The greater the sacrifice the greater the meaningfulness of the call."* It was then that I realized that my long testimony entailing my acceptance of Jesus Christ as the controller of my life and my dedication to my teaching job, which led to excellent results in exams, as well as my visible leadership talents, won me the hearts of the interviewing panel. The question of leaving my well-paying job and all other would-be promotions in favor of joining the Ministry was of paramount value to them. There was also the other aspect, unlike the other candidates who focused on the physical benefits of joining the Ministry, such as an opportunity to get a job, a channel to go overseas or one of those ways of being assured of owning a vehicle in one's life, my motivation was sincere and spiritually divine. The panel realized that I was so ignorant of all the other benefits, as I had very little knowledge about the Church, if any.

Now that I was in college, I embarked on living to my call. I wanted to go to the training because, among other things, to work unreservedly in the Lord's vineyard. I also wanted to learn theology as well as about the Presbyterian Church of East Africa, which I considered my Church right from birth. I embarked on learning all that pertains to the Presbyterian Church. Its Church constitution, known as the 'Practice and Procedure' became quite a focus in my studies. If I had two books in my hand, one of the two would be the Practice and Procedure. I read it to an extent of memorizing it. I also took every opportunity to learn from the ordained pastors, especially from the late Rev. Muchui and Students like the late Geoffrey Ngoima and the late Rev. Kibicho, who were well versed with the Presbyterian system. They were so willing to let me learn from them. We developed a very good friendship.

By the end of the first year, none surpassed me in the knowledge of Presbyterianism. I was already a reliable contributor to our Presbyterian students ' meeting s and the Presbyterianism group studies that met once a week. I excelled so much that I was appointed the chairman of the Presbyterian body in college. In my final year of college, I was elected the overall college students' body treasurer. I participated in many kinds of sports. I played soccer for the school. I also actively took part in volleyball and table tennis. My main challenger in the latter was Samuel Kinyua, a good friend who lived in the USA at the time. I had left my family at Mukungugu-Njoro, and I used to go home occasionally as I was limited in terms of getting bus fare. Fortunately, my parents lived in Gikambura, which was approximately 20 Km south of the college. Thus, I used to go there over the weekends.

As students, we lived under very difficult circumstances, especially when it came to transport. My student's allowance per month was only Ksh. 300 which, according to the exchange rate by then, was like 1 dollar to 10 shillings. Meaning I used to get $30 as a monthly allowance. Therefore, instead of going home, I opted to send that money to my wife who could then top up her minimal salary and helped in sustaining the family. It was a real struggle but my wife kept on encouraging me. She and the children were working hard to raise the food stuff from the garden. The good news is that in spite of the money scarcity,

I did not look back and desire the much money I used to get as a headmaster of both Primary and Secondary schools. Neither did I ever calculate how much money I would have been earning, especially the upgrading that would have taken place and the consequent promotion to Area Education Officer. My heart rejoiced in the hardships and the more I encountered them, the stronger my faith and my calling. Yes, I did miss going home as regularly as I would have liked, but that did not seem to be a hindrance to both my academic and spiritual journey.

Whenever I delayed my scheduled home visit, I would receive calls from my longing family. While my wife understood my situation, the children, in the real sense, did not understand. They immensely used to miss me because my home visit had a lot of significance. It involved the preparation and feasting of delicacies like chapatti or mandazi.

At St. Paul's, I made many friends with students of other denominations. One such was Kirombo Samboja, who was an Anglican from Taita. We developed such intimacy that my wife and I went all the way to Mombasa to be the best couple at their wedding. Another of our school mate was Kalu, who later became bishop of Mombasa Diocese. I also made friends among the teaching staff. Among them included Dr. Robert Anderson, the late Dr. Mutungi, my Greek Language teacher. Anderson hailed from Scotland. We had become quite good friends. He visited my home at

Mukungugu, Njoro. I have since then met him three times in Scotland. He used to jokingly call me 'Moderator' for he would tell me, *"You have the moderatorial talents."* But he would then laugh, and I would then jokingly say, *"Yours is the prophetic word, and I will not be surprised if one time I find myself being the Moderator of the General Assembly, heading the PCEA Church."* Then, we would laugh. The students took this nickname. They all called me *"Moderator."* This prophetic reality came to reality in April of 2003 when I was elected as the Moderator of the General Assembly, a position I held for six years.

Anderson was a senior bachelor, and I was really moved by the way he had a good moral life. Rev. Dr. Zablon Nthamburi was another very good friend. He taught my major subject, Church History. He handled the subject so majestically. Nthamburi's approach to teaching this subject motivated me even more. Nthamburi later became the Presiding bishop of the Methodist Church in Kenya. His taking this prominent position in one of the mainstream Churches in Kenya did not take me by surprise because he is such a fine, God-fearing person and very devoted as far as the promotion of God's kingdom is concerned.

History was a subject I looked forward to teaching if I ever got a chance to teach in a Theological School or schools. True to my desire, I have in the past taught history in many theological and academic institutions, including St. Paul's United Theological College (Now St. Paul's University),

Presbyterian College and Daystar University. History being my major, I decided to do a historical thesis. I researched 'The History of St. Paul's Theological College from 1930-1982,' which became quite classical research. This and the other studies kept me so busy that if one would have wanted to see me, he/she could only be directed either to the library or to my room. People knew me as a very studious person. I became so well versed in research work that in later years during my postgraduate studies, I managed to do extensive research on the History of the East African Revival Movement and The Introduction and Development of Education by the Presbyterians in Kenya. This kind of motivation was very important, for the workload at St. Paul's College called for in-depth studies. No wonder then, having started as a class of fifteen students, only eight of us completed. All the others failed in their examinations and they had to pack and go home. Among those who finished included me, Bilida Bagambo (from Rwanda), Kirikiru, Samboya, Odido, Jane Karuri, Ngotho and one more whom I cannot recall his name. After finishing our academic work in June 1983, we went to our respectful Churches to await graduation in October. The marking of the exam took time because it was done both locally and internationally.

MINISTRY AT THOGOTO PARISH

After finishing my studies at St Paul's United Theological College, the P.C.E.A Church Appointment Committee had me posted to Thogoto Parish. This was in accordance with the recommendation of the Training and Personnel Development Committee that I be posted not far from PCEA Pastoral Institute, where there was already an ongoing training of around eighty theological students. The committee emphasized the importance of my being a teacher at the Pastoral Institute, where there was a pressing need for a Church history teacher. As already hinted, the Church lacked such a person among the ordained clergy. For that reason, though it was against the Church tradition that theological students be taught by a person not ordained, the Church had no option but to involve me in teaching. In fact, the training committee had eagerly waited for the completion of my studies at St. Paul's so that I could be used in teaching this subject. The recommendation was that I be posted to a parish within or near the PCEA Pastoral Institute so that I may teach the Church history subject as a part-time lecturer. As stated, such a recommendation to teach students undergoing Ministry training was quite rare by then.

An un-ordained person would hardly teach theological students. It called for an ordained person with some experience in the parochial work in the Church so that the teaching could be contextualized and, therefore, applicable. This would be the kind of combination I would have preferred in my Church Ministry. That is, being involved in parochial work and also having a teaching engagement. This is the best combination that I would have dreamt of. The advantage I had over other people was that I was not only a trained teacher but an experienced headmaster. I began teaching Church history at P.C.E.A Pastoral Institute in July 1983. This teaching was not only good for the students but also for me. The students were really spiritual. From my teaching perspective, I could see that almost all of them had the call to serve God. They were devoted to their learning and were a very disciplined lot for God's vineyard. In them, I saw a potential manpower and God's army in the P.C.E.A Church. They greatly uplifted my faith in God and the desire to make disciples in them. They were very ready to throw the net on the other side of the boat for an abundant catch for the Lord. This greatly motivated me to teach them. In them, I had good friends. Likewise, in me, they felt they had a friend. It is in the rebirth of this atmosphere that I developed a cordial relationship with all my theological students and I have maintained the same relations all along. I have always valued the relationship we had with them and the support each one of us has developed over the years. Quite a number of them portrayed potential leadership qualities. Such included Githinji, Ndegwa, Bobby, Wairi, and Njoroge, among others. As for the parish life at Thogoto, I was placed under a very able Minister with great experience by the name of Edward Ndirangu Samson, commonly known as ENS. Edward celebrated his 50th anniversary in the Ministry in April 2002. Thus, by 1983, when I was placed under him, he had many years of experience. Edward had also grown up in the Presbyterian Church. His father, Samson, was the first African session clerk when the Church was known as the Church of Scotland Mission (CSM). This was the time when the Presbyterian Church in Kenya was regarded as not yet mature. It was not until 1955 that it was given autonomy. It became the Presbyterian Church of East Africa with its own General Assembly. The first African moderator of the church was Charles Kareri. Samson was also the first African to handle a dead body. In the African culture, it was taboo to touch a dead body because it was regarded as unclean, and anyone who could touch it would also be considered unclean and, therefore, undergo a very intense mandatory cleansing ceremony.

Samson was then one of those early spiritual children of the missionaries who opened the eyes of the Kikuyu tribe to the value of the human body. Thus, ENS was brought up in the life and the traditions of the P.C.E.A at Thogoto. He was a staunch defender of Scottish traditions. One of these traditions was the fact that there was not to be an emphasis on the role of the Holy Spirit in the Church. The worship was also to be carried out in a motionless mood, that is, with no movements or clapping of hands as people sang. Woe unto him who would have encouraged worship styles contrary to such piety in the Church. Everything was to be done decently and orderly. The elders were also to carry out their parochial duties cooperatively. There were not to be sections of membership allocated to individual elders. Thogoto Parish, by then, had five congregations that were widely scattered.

Edward exposed me to all advantageous ways of training. He used to sit with me to explain the best ways to handle the Ministry work especially on Scottish traditions. He claimed to have noticed some non-Presbytery traits in me. These traits were leaning towards the charismatic ways. He was a good mentor, but unfortunately, he could not separate me from the charismatic spirit. He exposed me to sharing the Kirk session meetings and other committees and also involved me in the funerals and weddings. I also taught Catechism class, especially to the children of Rev. Musa Gitau Primary School. I also made home visitations more so for the aged and the disadvantaged people. Some people used to refer to me as the pastor for the distressed people. And they were not wrong. That is one of my main passions. That is why in the later Ministry, the church at one time decided to post me to Mathare Parish (the second largest slum in Kenya) as many pastors posted there took it as a punishment or discredited it as humiliation. I, on the other hand, joyfully embraced it.

NEGLECTED

The only negative thing that I encountered during the practical training was the fact that I lived with my parents and I was not given any house allowance. This was contrary to the PCEA ways of treating a student on internship. Constitutionally, when a student is posted in a parish, the presbytery will make sure that before that person is invited, there is good housing, including all the required utilities. So, my case was taken lightly. There was a feeling among the Parish elders that I was not the kind of pastor they would have liked. First, my father was anti-colonial, something the elders hated, as many were imperial loyalists. There was also the feeling that I had come from outside the Thogoto area. Gikambura, where I had come from, was regarded as *"Gentile inhabited"* as people were not *"civilized."* There was also the fact that, I had come from a very poor family. For these reasons, I was despised and therefore neglected. I was living under the 600 shillings students' allowance. Yet, I had to visit my family in Njoro quite often. Without financial support, life became very difficult for me. In parish life, it was a tradition, that the Church groups and especially the women Guild be encouraged to visit the home of the student in practice and give support for maintenance in cash and in-kind, including food provisions.

This was not so in my case. In all the time I worked as a student at Thogoto Parish, I never had even one person, let alone groups visiting me where I lived. Many had the will, but the parish leadership blocked them. The elders never visited me. We were looked at as poor gentiles. The problem now was that three of my kids were already in school, and we had to pay for their uniforms, building funds, activities and school fees. It then happened that any time I went home, I would find a message from the headmaster that the school debts had to be cleared including the children being fitted with new uniforms. I would then visit the headmaster and plead with him not to expel the children, giving him some promise that I would do the necessary within a week or two. Unfortunately, nothing happened.

I remember a number of times when I went home and completely avoided meeting the headmaster. It became like a hide-and-seek game. But then, I came home one weekend, and the first thing my wife gave me was the letter from the headmaster. In part, the letter said,

"The School Committee met and they conclusively gave you only two weeks to clear the debt, failure to which your children will be sent home."

I then visited the headmaster to plead for more time, but he told me,

"You know, Mr. Githii, some of the members of the school Committee are very bitter with you. They claimed that these rules were there even when you were the headmaster of this school and that you, too, had a limit on school debt. They,

therefore, came to the conclusion that no more sympathy should be extended to you. In this case, I have my hands tied up. I can no longer help. I understand, but they don't understand. Let us hope something will happen between now and then."

That was the worst experience for me since joining the Ministry. It would be a very painful experience to have my children sent home. This would make me a laughing stock for those who had expressed doubt that opting to join the Holy Ministry, thus leaving a very well-paying job, was a clear indication that I was out of my mind. The other side of the problem was that I could not highlight my problem to the parish leaders or members. If I did that, the elders would have quickly taken the advantage to interpret that as a weakness on my side. Terming it as a reflection of my lack of perseverance or a sign of greed for money, hence, I had to be very cautious and not let anyone in the parish learn about my problem. There were many times I failed to go home for lack of bus fare, but I could not communicate this to any Church leader because it would have seemed like I was asking for money from the Church members. The truth of the matter was that almost all parish leaders had their eyes on me looking for anything to accuse me of.

It was while in this dilemma, wondering where my help was to come from, that the Holy Spirit led me to Psalm 121, which says, *"I lift up my eyes to the hills...where does my help come from? My help comes from the Lord, the maker of heaven and earth..."* It is then that I decided now to plead my case to the Lord. I got an empty sack, folded it and placed it next to my bed. Being on my knees was the first thing I did after coming out of bed for three days. Each time I prayed, I dialogued with God through Jesus Christ. I reminded Him of all the people who openly said that something was wrong with my head when I chose to join the Holy Ministry. I told God to remember how these people called me a fool for opting to go to the Ministry at a time when I enjoyed leadership as headmaster of primary and several secondary schools. I had been widely respected and was awaiting promotions. I reminded God that I did sacrifice all that in order to serve Him. I would ask him questions to Him like,

> *"What do you think these people will say of me? Are they not going to say that their prophesies were correct because as they had predicted that my life and that of my family would be doomed as it was happening now? Is this not a way of giving the devil the carpet to glorify himself?"*

In my dialogue with the Lord, I always assured Him that I did not doubt His ability. I would tell Him that I still remembered and believed in what He did through Moses by creating a highway in the Red Sea despite Pharaoh's fast-approaching soldiers. On the same note, I reminded Him of the fact that He could feed 5,000 women and children when the situation was too desperate even to his disciples. Every evening and morning, I dialogued with the Lord but in the humblest position of kneeling. After each time I prayed, I felt so relieved and relaxed.

I slept deeply and went about my daily engagements with ease. I did this for some time. One day, having prayed, taken a shower and breakfast, I headed for the Church office. At the Church of the Torch, I had to walk for about five miles. Sometimes, I had to walk very fast in order to make it to the office in time. I did not want to give the parish minister a loophole to write a negative report on me or talk ill of me in the Kirk session or presbytery meeting. I would have boarded a bus, but I could hardly afford it. That day, I was a bit late, and I walked faster. No sooner had I arrived in the office than Njeri, the Secretary - said to me, *"David, there is a letter for you here."* I picked up the letter, looked at the envelope and the writing on it indicated that the letter was from PCEA Church Head Office. The immediate thoughts that came to my mind were that the letter meant a transfer to another place. I was, therefore, reluctant to open the letter, but I had to open it anyway. Upon opening and spreading it, I could not believe my eyes. The letter carried the good news that the finance committee of the Church had, in one of its committee meetings, decided to increase the salaries of the ministers and Church workers.

I do not remember the percentage of increase, but the letter went on to say that the increment had been backdated seven months and further indicated that the said amount of money shown in the letter was already in my bank account. What good news, and what better way for God to have answered my prayers. The words that my wife said as I consulted her for my going to the Ministry back in 1979 echoed through my mind, *"These children will not miss food, education or clothing."* As I read the letter, the ENS entered into the office. I did not waste time. I just went to him, and not really wanting to expose my problems, I asked him for permission to go home, claiming I had an urgent matter to attend to. He replied,

> *"I am not ignorant to the fact that you have a home and children to take care of. Next time you have something urgent to handle in regard to your family, please, just go, but let me know where you are by leaving the message, either written or verbal, with the secretary."*

I found this kind of arrangement as favour from God. The ENS had not been kind to me all the time, especially after I had asked for the provision of a house. I left and walked to Gitaru (about five miles from the Church office), boarded a bus and arrived at Nakuru by around 2.00 pm.

I then went straight into the Kenya National Bank, where my bank account was. I asked for the balance, and true to the Church letter, the money was already in the bank account. I withdrew enough money to meet all that was required at the school. I also made adequate provisions for domestic use. I left quite a substantial amount of money in the account. I went, paid the school fees then I did some shopping and proceeded home.

In the course of my first few months at Thogoto Parish, I became well-known. This was mainly through my involvement in parish life, especially through the visits to the aged, the needy, and the bereaved and preaching in Church groups, especially the women's guild. Thus, when my graduation came in October of that year, 1983, the entire Thogoto Parish was virtually involved in one way or the other. Every Parish member of the women's guild adorning their women's guild head-scarves came for the graduation. They dominated the entire graduation ceremony. The climax came when my name was called out. The women shouted in joy and, at the same time, clapped their hands while singing. As soon as the graduation ceremony was over, the community of Thogoto parish flooded the ground took over. They sang songs in praise of God as well as congratulating me for that achievement. After my graduation, I went on with my duties at Thogoto Parish where I persistently pushed for the establishment of Elder Districts.

THE ORIGIN OF ELDER DISTRICTS IN PCEA CHURCH

The most memorable work at Thogoto Parish, which has come in the course of years to be embraced by the whole denomination, is the Ministry of the small Church groups in the Church that I called, *'The Elder Districts.'* The idea of applying the functioning of the Church through small groups originated from my involvement in running the schools' sports in small groups. I had sub-divided my school into small groups known as *'Houses.'* In using this method, I was able to produce the best sports men and girls to represent my schools in soccer, netball and athletics. I used the same method in teaching. I would have the class divided into small groups that worked together in the undertaking of all subjects. In this way, the weak students were uplifted by the knowledgeable ones. In the lower school, the classes worked through small groups known as 'New Primary Approach.' This approach was based on subdividing the pupils into small groups. This made it possible for the teacher and the good pupils to help the weaker pupils. It is this idea of making schools to operate in small groups that I felt compelled by the Holy Spirit to introduce into the Church. This is the very time I was a theological student under practical teaching in Thogoto Parish.

First, I decided to share the idea with the parish minister under whom I was being trained for parochial work. This was in early 1984. To my surprise, his first reaction was very negative, for he said,

"We have never done that in PCEA. Furthermore, it sounds to be a very divisive idea. How can you dare to disrupt a parish that has survived so cohesively over many years? Such a move would even make it hard for the presbytery to qualify you for ordination. There is no way I can allow such an agenda to be floated in a Kirk session meeting."

The Minister's negative response made me feel like it was a sign of not only rejecting me but also rejecting a beautiful child that God was birthing in the PCEA Church. Nevertheless, the Holy Spirit kept on urging me to pursue the idea. He spoke to me through God's Word in Isaiah 41: 10-11,

"I will strengthen you and help you; I will uphold you with my righteous right hand. All who rage against you will surely be ashamed and disgraced."

I did not then give up. Then there was this time I organized a seminar for the elders of Rev. Musa Gitau Memorial Church. It was one of the five congregations in Thogoto Parish. It was then that I took the opportunity to introduce the functioning of an Elder District. But in doing this I was to be very careful not to be seen as if I was going against the Parish Minister's warning that I dare not initiate that idea of Elder Districts. I also had to come up with teachings that could finally convince the elders of the importance of starting the so-called Elder District Movement. So, I had to make a very discreet move through biblical references.

Having gone through the seminar, I brought out an idea, suggesting to them that I would be willing to visit a number of members in their homes for prayers on a particular day. In doing this, I would prefer that I be accompanied by an elder and some deacons and that it would look awkward when all elders and all deacons accompanied me as we moved from one house to another. I told them for this to work, we had to subdivide the congregation membership among the elders, each taking a certain area in the neighborhood and being its caretaker. This neighborhood area would take the name Elder District. Thus, the day I was to visit, I would be accompanied by the elders and the deacons in that area. I also convinced them that it would also be easier if members in each locality had to address all their concerns to the elder manning their elder district who would then forward their concerns to the congregation's local council. This meant that if a member needed a child to be baptized, such a member would inform the elder overseeing the area in which one resided. This idea was well received by the majority of the elders and deacons. We, therefore, came up with a program tabulating the way I was to visit the Elder Districts accompanied by one elder manning the district and the deacon within that elder district. We also agreed to give specific names to each of the districts according to their location or just a Biblical name. I became very active in visiting the individual homes, and soon, I was through with that. Next, I came up with a common song which I assigned the Elder Districts to practice and then sing in a competition on a set day. On this day, each group took the floor before adjudicators.

There were marks awarded for the style of the entry, the arrangement, the accompaniments and their use, as well as the costumes. 50% was awarded for the actions applied in singing. There were also marks awarded for the way the group left the stage in exit after the presentation.

One of the things I aimed at discouraging was the style of singing inherited from the Scottish Church traditions. I was after reclaiming the old African style of singing, which involved a lot of movements. The Scottish Missionaries referred to this as 'Pagan' and non-Presbyterian. I was reminded more and more of the way David is biblically referred to as having sung for the Lord until his clothes loosened to the point of falling down. The aim of doing all this was to create an atmosphere conducive to people fellowshipping and laughing together as they practiced. It was a catalyst to pull them to come together. People have to have an agenda if they have to come together. There have also to be deadlines set to create urgency and importance of the meeting. This move is especially important in the initial stages of organizing small groups. Something has to be there to act like a vehicle for all to travel together.

The other phase I involved the districts in was the program that paved the room for the groups' fellowship every Wednesday. The aim was to make all the Church or most of its members meet in between the Sundays. This helped the members to feel that they belonged, as each member felt the warmth of the others while sharing in prayers and concerns, reading the Word together, singing, and sharing in joy and sorrow.

It was an avenue for discipleship. The Wednesday fellowship turned out to be a good avenue to train and equip Christians. The members learnt how to read the Bible to fight out fear. They learnt to express themselves, pray and share in the joy and sorrow of others. This ministry that started like a mustard seed has, at the writing of this book, become a big tree where the P.C.E.A Church has built nests of rapid Church growth, spiritual maturity, and cohesiveness in Church membership. This has increased giving in the church and enhanced more involvement of the elders. It has also paved the way for the adults and the young to come together and, by so doing, greatly reduce the generational gap. The area dealing with the initiation of Elder Districts will be elaborated on in detail later in this book.

The year 1984, therefore, saw me accomplish many things at Thogoto Parish, which comprised the Church of the Torch, Rev. Musa Gitau Memorial Church, PCEA Ondiri Church, PCEA Rusigiti Church and the Renguti Church. Since then, the former Thogoto Parish has been subdivided into Thogoto Parish, Rev. Musa Gitau Parish, Mai-a-Ihii Parish and Rusigiti Parish. The then South Kiambu

Presbytery, where Thogoto Parish was incorporated, has since then been subdivided into Kikuyu Presbytery, Limuru Presbytery, Githunguri Presbytery, Kambui Presbytery and the subdividing continues....

DELAYED ORDINATION

Meanwhile, my persistent in the establishment of the Elder Districts did not augur well in the presbytery circles. It challenged the Scottish traditions and revealed the truth about the scriptures. The issue of the possibility of my being licensed as a clergyman, which would then lead to ordination, kept on surfacing in the Presbytery meetings that took place every three months. According to the PCEA constitution, one is supposed to be licensed after six months of practical work. When that time came, the presbytery withheld my licensing, accusing me of being a divisive person, one who would go and dismantle Church systems by introducing what I called *'Elder Districts'* and also introducing ways that would incorporate the movement of the Holy Spirit in the Church. There was also the introduction of praise and worship sessions, which created much unease in the leadership of the church. As time went on, the situation worsened as I was accused of having created *"sub-Churches"* at Musa Gitau memorial Church. Yet, the worst was to come.

Towards the end of two years, after I got into that parish, the presbytery called for a special presbytery meeting whose main agenda was to declare that I never be ordained as PCEA Church minister; hence, I was to be blocked from being ordained and therefore kicked out of Thogoto Parish. By God's grace, the then moderator of the General Assembly, the Very Reverend Dr. George Wanjau, learnt of the summoning by the South Kiambu presbytery to disown me. He quickly called the officials of the South Kiambu Presbytery and appealed to them to change their minds. Upon their resistance, he entered into a memorandum of understanding that they ordain me, and as per the stand of officials, I would then be posted under a very senior clergyman to mentor me into real Presbyterianism. They argument was that I seemed to carry some 'Pentecostal influence in the works of the Holy Spirit'. This is why they accused me of having a custom of teaching members of the Church to sing *"Nyimbo cia Kiroho"* (Holy Spirit-related songs), which was considered outlawed in the PCEA Church. The GA Moderator agreed to the memorandum. On October 21, 1984, my licensing took place at the Church of the Torch. The licensing was marked by a lot of joy from all members of Thogoto Parish. All congregations were closed for that Sunday so that all members could converge at the Church of the Torch which is also known as Kimuri. Kimuri is a Kikuyu name for 'Torch.' This Church, which was constructed between 1928 and 1933, acquired this name as it was seen as the source of spiritual light to all other parts of Kenya. It is important to understand that, before the coming of the Missionaries from Europe and America, Africa was referred to as *"The Dark Continent."*

This was not the physical light as Africa is divided into two portions by the Equator. It meant the spiritual light. Until the 19th Century, the Gospel of Jesus Christ had not penetrated into Africa. Each group of people had their own way of honoring what to them was a supernatural power. My tribe, the Kikuyus, talked of the supernatural power as 'Ngai', which meant 'one who provides.' Like the Jews, they believed in Jehovah Jireh. They believed that 'Ngai' lived on top of Mount Kenya (17,000ft), which was snow-capped. Since none of them had ever climbed the mountain, yet they could see that brightness at the apex of the mountain, they figured out that the brightness, which reached their eyes as a reflection of sunlight, meant that God's purity was the one that reached their eyes. To them, none else could attain such brightness apart from God. My people also believed that when God decided to come much nearer to the people, He stepped on the ground through the fig tree. This is a gigantic tree that is ever-green (The Mugumo tree). The Kikuyus equated this tree with God's might and its ever-greenness with the ever-living God. During a time of catastrophes like an epidemic or long drought, the very aged Kikuyu men sacrificed a lamb without blemish under this tree. They sprinkled the base of the fig tree with the blood from the animal, roasted and ate some of the meat (as sharing the meal with God) and then left the other meat under that tree, believing that God would come down and instead pour blessings to them. Now that the missionaries had come with the new revelation to Kikuyus that the last Lamb was slain, the forever-forgiving blood was shed, and the curtain in the temple was torn, making it possible for individuals to access God, these sacrificial lambs offered under the fig tree were no longer needed. The torch, which was the base or the source of the good news to radiate the new light, the new revelation, and lighten up all the dark corners of East Africa, was now introduced. The Holy Spirit was likened to the batteries of a torch and Presbyterianism to the torch itself. God was handling and directing the torch, and Jesus Himself was the light. This background of the Church of the Torch made my heart puffed up with joy when I realized that the act of licensing me and placing a white collar on my neck signified that I was another torch. The licensing mandated me to spread the light to the hearts of many people who lived in darkness.

The Holy Spirit was to empower me, God was to direct me and the Word in John 1 that this light was there before the beginning of creation was to enlighten my way. As the service went on, my mind was grazing back to 1979. It was like a tape running in my mind. I could recall all that seemed to be satanic confusion as I was undergoing my call. The way things happened fast, enticing me not to go to the ministry but to enjoy the fruits of promotions, the letter inviting me to the interview and Kirikiru forgetting to take His share and hence revert the catastrophe about it. Then there was the timely way I voiced my concern about that letter in the staff room, only for Kirikiru to go and get it from his coat.

What if Kirikiru was not there when I raised my concern? What if he was in the class or out of the school that day? What if he even never remembered since he was handed the letter at a time when his mind was very preoccupied? But worse still, what if I got the bus to take me home? I remembered the time I had figured out that I was so much of a fool to do the interview. What if I was nervous that time when I sat in front of the interviewing panel? But of paramount importance, what if I had never confessed Jesus Christ as my Lord and Savior on that remarkable day of October 31st 1976? Many 'what ifs' travelled in the path of my mind, even as I continued to follow the proceeds of the service. Finally, the collar was placed on me and immediately, I was pronounced as 'The Reverend David Muhia Githii.' This was followed by a prolonged clapping and the singing of the East African Revival Song *"Tukutendereza."* The moderator of the presbytery who licensed me gave me a lengthy piece of advice, and while I cannot remember it all, I still hear the eco of his voice saying to me,

> *"To be licensed to be a priest equals being given a towel to wash people's feet. It should never be confused with the stick and the hat that is given to the chief on the day of installation. The priest is a servant, and the chief is a boss. Rev. David Githii, note the difference."*

This piece of advice has ever lived with me. There are those moments that like all human beings, I tend to drift away, but this statement has always brought me right to the track. The towel image has many times acted as the light at the tower to guide me, just as the Light House light guides the ship or the plane heading to its destination. My ordination quickly followed. It took place at PCEA Kamandura. This was one of those early mission stations that the pioneer missionaries opened. It is about 20 miles from Kimuri Church. Other spots included Rungiri and Ngeca. To be ordained in such a spot reminded me that I was not meant to be stationed in one place; my call had to be mobile. It was easier to be licensed and ordained at Kimuri, but God found it important that I get out of the four walls of Kimuri. In fact, at Kamandura, my ordination, together with the other three candidates took place outside the sanctuary. The sanctuary was too small to contain the huge number of people who turned up from Thogoto Parish, Ngeca Parish, Rungiri Parish and others from Meru (200 miles away). This was particularly so because of Isaac Mpungu, who was as well-being ordained and hailed from Meru. Other candidates for ordination included Lenard Kimani and another person from Maasai land. The ordination of a Maasai tribe person was important for the Church since, for a long time, the PCEA Church had so much emphasized on training the Kikuyu and Meru tribes for the Ministry. This was limiting outreach to other tribes in Kenya because among other reasons, these were not able to speak the language of the people they evangelized to. They were also not able to contextualize the message. Thus, for a Maasai person to be ordained was an important step towards reaching out to the Maasai tribe.

Our ordination was conducted by the then moderator of the General Assembly, The Rt. Rev. John Gatu. He happened to be one of the long-serving PCEA church leaders. He is a person who, in many ways, had spearheaded the growth of this Church in all its dimensions of growth, especially in its physical and spiritual growth. He had been the Church Secretary General for 18 years and the moderator of the General Assembly for 6 years. He was a Church leader greatly admired in all circles of the Church. Again, to be ordained by John was of great importance to me. But I also learned later that he was a very controversial person especially when it came to treasuring the Scottish tradition upon which the PCEA Church was founded. In later years, we had to differ a lot when I became the Moderator of the General Assembly. Prior to ordination, John Gatu had given me some words of advice. His advice falls among those things you hear and hardly forget. His words of advice came from Acts 27:1- 26. This was the time Paul was being transported to Rome where he had made the appeal to the Supreme Court. On the way, he and the crew faced a lot of sea calamities. Likewise, Gatu told me that by entering into Holy Ministry, I had registered for persecution and hardship.

Prophetically, Gatu talked of my future persecution for the gospel. But like Paul who was rescued many times by God, I would likewise, be many times rescued from wicked men's hands. History proved his words true, though he also turned out to be one of my persecutors. The ordination day on December 30th 1984, turned up to be a very cold day. This kind of weather is dominant in the Limuru area but this Sunday was terribly cold. This reminded me of that cold night that made Peter warm himself near the fire as the trial of Jesus continued - it was as he warmed himself that he denied Jesus three times. Thus, as the service developed, I was at one time meditating on how much I should always warm myself in the Spirit of God. Remembering John Gatu's advice from Acts 27, I am always reminded that there are to be cold days in my path of ministry, but at whatever cost, I have to persistently work in season and out of season and at no time should I ever deny Jesus Christ in spite of the obstacles. My call and ordination should be a pointer to the path of my ministry. There was no better affirmation of the accomplishment of my call than that moment when my coat was removed, and three Ministers were busy, first dressing me with the cassock and then belting me, then the dressing with the gown, the hood and the scarf. The joy in the act of ordination was mixed with sorrow, the sorrow of feeling the heavy burden that was now placed on my shoulders. I remembered the way Jesus struggled with the cross to Calvary and the way Simon of Cyrene was forced by the Roman soldiers to carry it. I remembered Jesus' Word, *"Whoever... should deny himself and follow me."* The concern that I had to deny myself and, unlike Simon carry the cross willingly made my joy to be overshadowed by the sorrow. Nevertheless, the words that were being sung by the congregation as I was being dressed in the robe was energizing my heart. It was a song I had come to like very much. It was not my choice, but the Holy Spirit should have led one person among the ministers to start that hymn which was then picked by the entire congregation. It was

Relentless Life Bumps

hymn number 292 from the Kikuyu language version,
Nyimbo cia Kiroho. The song went like this:

Unyite na guoko njikarage nawe
Ndikuiire muti wakwa wa kwambirwo
Njikarage nawe mathina – ini mothe
Nige th a u nde ith ie ku hot an a

Mwathani ni njui ndukandiga
Naningwenda ngona riri wa matu- ini
Uhithe o haria thu itanginyona
Ungiona uuru uhithe

(Hold up my hand
While I carry the Cross of crucifixion.
That I abide with you in all hostile
Encounters
 so that you will help me to overcome
God, I know you will never abandon me
My focus is to witness your glory in heaven
Hide me where the enemy cannot trace me.
When you see evil, hide me)

Na nii nunjui ndiri hinya Mwathani
(I am aware I have no strength of my own)
Wa gwitiririria nditi cia Shaitani
(To overcome the satanic torrents)
Na thuti cia mwiri na wendo wa arata
(And the evil desires and friends love)
Na miago ya thi itari bata
(And all hopeless earthly attraction)

Mwathani ninjui kuri hindi igoka
(One thing am aware of is that a time is coming)
Ugatwara andu aku iguru makahuruke
(You receive your people into your Kingdom to rest.)
Undeithie gutiga mihang'o ya thi ino
(Help me to overcome the earthly pressures)
Niguo hotage gwithagathaga
(That I will be in a position to prepare myself)
Ndarikia gukinya mucii ucio wa iguru
(When finally, I get into heaven)
Shaitani ndagacoka guthinia ringi.
(The devil will have no way to manipulate my life)
Baba ni akahimbiria na moko make
(God will embrace me with his hands)
Ahurukie wendo – ini wake.
(And make me restful in his Eternal love)

As the hymn drew to a close, so was the dressing, and then there was a thunderous singing of *"Tukutendereza,"* and then came the sermon. The Rt. Rev. John Gatu delivered the sermon that really uplifted my spirit. He emphasized that on His eve of exit, Jesus mandated the disciples to go into the whole world and gave them the authority to teach and baptize, and of more significance, He promised to be with them always. Thus, he reminded us that God had a purpose in each one of us and as a pilot directs the plane guided by a compass, despite the height and the clouds, God will pilot us over and above all stumbling blocks in the path of our ministry.

Ours was to keep the spiritual ears open so that the devil would not block it. Sometimes, God does not speak to us in a thunderous kind of communication. Sometimes, He does so to us in whispers, sometimes using people like children, illiterate members of our society, very aged members, through the parish session, youth, choirs, a theological student and even other ministers. As he put it,

"It all means keeping your spiritual ears open, bearing in mind that we are fighting with the principalities of darkness."

He finished by quoting the book of Joshua 1:9,

"Have I not commanded you, do not be terrified, do not be discouraged. For the Lord your God will be with you always wherever you go."

This last biblical reference has always motivated me in my Ministry. There are those times, I feel like getting terrified and discouraged, but the promise that the Lord will be with me wherever I go has many a time uplifted me. A few days before the ordination, I received a letter indicating that I had been transferred to Nakuru Parish with effect from January 2nd 1985. Thus, even as the ordination was being carried out, I knew that my work at Thogoto Parish had come to an end. And true to the South Kiambu Presbytery stand, no sooner had I got ordained on December 30th than I reported at Nakuru Parish which is around 100 miles from Thogoto.

MINISTRY AT NAKURU PARISH

Sure enough, in January 1985, I reported to Nakuru Parish, which was manned by Rev. Gibbon Kirathi, formerly a senior chief with the Kenyan Government. I was, therefore, under his mercy. He was mandated by the Church to straighten me by instilling the real Presbyterian spirit in me. He was also to drain out the spirit of Pentecostalism in me. He was also to make sure that that spirit in me, which was advocating the subdivision of congregations into Elder Districts, got defused. He was to restrain me from teaching and encouraging members of the Church to sing *"Kiroho songs"* (Praise in Worship). At Nakuru Parish, Rev. Kirathi was the sole minister. This Parish had 32 congregations, with Dr. Arthur memorial Church being the parish headquarters. Rev. Kirathi was another experienced minister, having received his call as he served in his secular job as a chief at Ngeca in Kiambu Presbytery. I admired his parochial and presbytery administration. He was a person who had managed to put down the chief's hat and the rod of authority, replacing them with a towel and stooping down to servanthood. He received me very well. He seemed to understand that I was really green as my ordination was not even a week old. He, therefore, carefully helped me administrate the Holy Communion, baptisms, office administration and carrying out the daily schedules of a minister in a big town like Nakuru.

Yes, the culture of the people was quite different from the one of Thogoto, where the Parishioners were farmers and others working in Nairobi, some commuting to work every day. Rev. Kirathi very lovingly introduced me to the culture of the Nakuru Kirk Session, which was very different from Thogoto Kirk Session, which was quite rigid in matters of spirituality, contrary to the Nakuru Parish, which was more relaxed. Kirathi kept a firm grip on me. Unlike the Thogoto parishioners, Nakuru residents were business people who were not easily reached during the day. My other Ministry involved visiting people's homes, one of the things that was highly opposed. At that time, the home visitation Ministry did not exist. The Ministry was confined to the Church and the office. However, I had an added advantage. It was this same town where I had nights of drinking alcohol during my headmastership at Barut Rhoda school. I, therefore, knew this town in and out. It was also at this PCEA Dr. Arthur Church that I first came when I was thirsting for the Word of God.

Yes, after the night I had spent at Sabab, after being left by my drunkard friends. I had found myself yearning for a relaxed life through a lasting connection with Jesus Christ. It was this Church I had attended almost three times, awaiting the altar call that never happened. It was from this same Church that Mr. Gatawa and Maina had come to visit me in my home at Langalanga estate, convincing me to surrender my life to Jesus Christ, but I felt I needed to claim my redemption not in the witness of two people but in a crowd of witnesses. For that reason, I declined to accept salvation at that time. This is the Church that I was now ministering in after ten years. I also felt my being in this town as a good opportunity for me to reach out to those with whom I used to drink with in the town. It was in Nakuru Parish, with its 32 congregations, that I decided to explore the ministry of elder Districts. One of the things that helped me greatly was the oneness of the Nakuru Parish Session and their understanding. I stayed under Rev. Kirathi for three months, after which, due to some unavoidable circumstances, he was transferred to Eldoret. Another senior clergy, Stephen Kariuki took his place. It was necessary to bring another senior clergy to manage me as provided for in the memorandum of understanding between South Kiambu Presbytery and PCEA Head Office. Stephen had been the moderator of the Western Presbytery prior to his transfer, and he had already been assigned to lead a delegation from that presbytery to their established partnership with some Churches in Germany. Thus, things seemed to work in my favour because no sooner had Stephen reported to Nakuru Presbytery than he had to proceed for leave as well as to Germany.

Rev. Nyutu Muhia was assigned to oversee the Nakuru parish during the time Stephen was to be absent. This happened despite his being the Minister at Gilgil parish, which had more than twenty congregations. Moreover, Gilgil Parish was fifty miles from Nakuru Parish. What the presbytery members did not know was that Rev Nyutu was on my side. He understood the value the idea of Elder Districts could add in promoting the entire denomination in many sectors of its life. He also liked the depth of my spirituality. He had no problem with *"Nyimbo cia Kiroho."* He, therefore, devised away in which I could be in charge of Nakuru Parish in the absence of Rev. Stephen. He organized the Nakuru Kirk session meeting, knowing very well that he would not chair the meeting. Thus, the day the meeting was to take place, early in the morning, he called the Nakuru Parish Session Clerk, informed him of his unavailability and asked him to have me chair the meeting. When the Session members met and received the information that Nyutu was not to come, they had no otherwise but to have me moderate it. I, therefore, took the position of Kirk Session Moderator.

On the agenda items presented for the meeting, I added one more on *"Elder Districts."* When we finally came to this agenda, I educated the elders on what I meant by Elder Districts, including the merits. Without much ado, they accepted the idea. They immediately embraced it, terming it as a wonderful catalyst for Church growth. We formulated a way on how the congregations were to be split into these small groups. Wednesday was set as the day when these groups would be holding the fellowship meetings. It was also emphasized that in every congregation I ministered on particular Sundays, I had to hold a meeting with both elders/deacons after the service so as to educate them further. The deacons, in particular, had to digest the idea that I would be making home visits every Sunday. It was also important that I let the leaders understand the protocols that needed to be observed during those times I would be making visits to the individual Elder Districts. At the same time, I had to explain the importance of the availability of the leaders during such visitations. It was also necessary for them to always have their ears open for any concern or joy among their members. If there were any issues, then they would go there without delay to pray and share in the experience with that particular family.

ELDER DISTRICT COMPETITIONS

By the time Stephen returned from Germany, he was shocked to learn that I had been manning the parish since his departure. He ventured into asking why the earlier arrangement that Rev. Nyutu is in charge was not honored, but he met resistance from the elders who came to the defense of both Rev Nyutu and myself. He then had no option but to recommend and support the Elder Districts movement. Now that Stephen had accepted this movement, and more so being both the parish minister and the moderator of the presbytery, I felt so much energized to mobilize the leaders and the congregations to have this movement fully instilled in their Church life. In doing this, I had great help from Mr. Geoffrey Nyaga Gathuku who was the parish Evangelist. This joint effort created a deep intimacy between me and Nyagah. I used to call him Timothy, my coworker, and he called me Paul, his coworker. He was one of my very close friends over the years. He resided in Seattle, USA, until his death in 2022. He was one of my closest friends for many years. This time round, I decided to move the Elder District Movement to another level. The means was to create a way through which there would be strong ties and cohesiveness among the individual district members. I convinced the elders to set a competitive mood among the people. This would be achieved through creating a task for each district to act on and in a set time. All the Elder Districts would come together for competition. Both the elders and the parish minister gave me a green light on this. I then picked hymn number 311 from "*Nyimbo cia Kiroho*" and a drama. Both of these set pieces were based on the Gospel of Mathew 25: 1-3, which talks of the ten virgins, five of whom were foolish and the other five wise. The marks for the song were allocated according to entry, arrangement, accompaniments and their use. The actions carried 50%, that is, the flow of the song, costumes and the way the group left the stage. The drama was to take 15 minutes.

For three months, the more than 100 Elder Districts became a beehive of activities. Every district was meeting as regularly as possible. In order to attract both children and men (who would be reluctant to join such activities) there were 15 marks awarded: 5 marks for the children's representations and 10 marks for men's representations. The latter was important for me because men are reluctant to come to the Church, and those who do are very slow in being involved in Church participation. I was looking for a way that would make the women, the children and the youth persuade their husbands, fathers and men neighbors to join them in these activities and help gain marks in that area. In doing so, some men would end up coming to the Church and also others who did come to the Church would find themselves involved actively in the life of the Church. This was Evangelism in disguise.

2.DEDICATION OF PCEA RUGURU CHURCH

It then happened that the officials of the General Assembly, Dr. George Wanjau and Plawson Kuria were coming to dedicate PCEA Ruguru Church in Nakuru Parish. The Presbytery, through its moderator Stephen, recommended that the best performers in the Ten Virgins' drama and hymn be placed in the program to perform during the dedication of Ruguru Church. As expected, these items were so polished that many viewers cried, especially during the drama. Dr Wanjau, the Moderator of the General Assembly and Plawson Kuria openly shed tears. These officials tried to inquire from those sitting next to them as to how all this came to happen. They were told that this movement, known as Elder Districts, was my brainchild, and it was only me who could explain how all this had been knit together. It was then, immediately after the service, that the GA Officials approached me and had me explain to them what all this meant.

The word 'Elder District,' was foreign to the entire denomination. This was my own invention. These GA Officials were so excited about this movement and, therefore encouraged me to push the idea ahead. They promised to help me in my endeavors. I remember the GA Moderator saying,

"This is a great pearl for this Church. If the same idea can permeate in the whole denomination, the Church would never be the same again."

Looking at me, he further said,

"Please, David, do your best to make this movement penetrate in the Church. On our side, we will do all we can to energize you."

Rev. Stephen Kariuki had joined me in the parish by April. He found me totally involved in the Elder District activities. It was not something he had experienced before, but after I explained it to him, he embraced the idea, and he gave me all the necessary back up. Kariuki was another experienced minister. He had come from a very humble background. He started by being an employee of a missionary teacher at St. Paul's United Theological College. He didn't have a profound education, but his missionary employer helped him learn. Kariuki was a brilliant person, and he finally had enough education to join St Paul's United Theological College as a theological student. After his graduation, Kariuki became a very able minister. Until his retirement in April 2002, he had served the PCEA Church in many capacities, especially as the moderator of many presbyteries and as a member of many key national Church committees, including the Business Committee, Appointment Committee, General Administrative Committee and was commissioner to many General Assemblies. Working under him in 1985 at Nakuru Parish was a great blessing to me. I again learnt a lot from him. In September 1985, I decided to give other items to the Elder Districts to practice. The fruits of the first one were so visible, among them being the way it had acted as a catalyst to bring people together. In fact, it had fulfilled among the members of each district what the psalmist said in Psalm 133, "*How good and pleasant it is when brothers live together in unity…*" It was also visible that this warmth from the elder district activities and the accompanying fellowship was being felt in the entire parish. The participatory mood of the members, including men, had increased. There was increased love and the spirit of forgiveness and the giving had increased too. The number of tithers and the increasing amount of money in other giving had increased. There was an increased interaction of people in a friendlier way.

PILGRIM'S PROGRESS

Not long after the Ten Virgins drama and song, the excitement had calmed down when some elders approached me and requested that I come up with other items for further competition. I then present this request to the Kirk Session meeting chaired by the parish minister. It was unanimously accepted. They all voted in favour of the request. This time, again, I needed to come up with an item that would motivate the members to fight the good fight in their spiritual journey and, at the same time, bring a more harmonizing spirit among the members. The Lord put in my mind the work of John Bunyan in his book, Pilgrim's Progress. I instructed the Elder Districts first to read the book, noting the characters, the scenes and the various teachings represented in that book. After this, the districts were to compose a 15-minute play and a six-stanza song without a chorus from the same book. The song was to be composed and sung in the style of an African folk song. This turned out to be a very exciting experience for all the members of the parish.

The Pilgrim's Progress book was so much sought after by the bookshops in Nakuru Town, such that its original price rose from 12 to 18 Kenya shillings. By applying the same approach to the competitions all the way from congregational to zonal and finally parish level, I managed to come up with a very refined play and song demonstrating the Christian journey from the doomed city to heaven. This included all the challenges he encountered along the way. By December 1985, the competitions were concluded. These two items, *'The Ten Virgins'* and *'The Pilgrim's Progress,'* left Nakuru Parish with very high spiritual wealth and vibrating with eagerness to work for the Lord. The Membership had also greatly increased because, through the competitions. The Elder District members reached out to people of all ages to come and give them a push to get a good position within the Elder District competition line up. There were those who came as spectators but finally opted to become members of the Church. As I was organizing these end-of-the-year Elder District activities, I had already received a letter transferring me to Rongai Parish. This was towards the end of November.

Rongai Parish was adjacent to Nakuru Parish. In fact, the Rongai Parish minister's house was located in Nakuru Parish. The parish headquarters was at St. Ninian's Church, which was located at Nakuru showground, which was also in Nakuru Town. This being the case, I was actually not really moving out of Nakuru Parish. My presence was to be experienced very often because I had to interact with the members all the time. Rongai Parish had 20 congregations. It extended from Nakuru Town to Makutano which would be about 60 miles. 80% of the congregations in the Rongai Parish were in remote places, and some were located in forested areas like Sabatia, Icagiri, Kampi ya Moto, Maji Mazuri and others. For nine years, this Parish had failed to complete its assessed money by the Church General Assembly through the presbytery. Apart from the people who were part of the Kiamunyi, Menengai, Rongai Kampi ya Moto, and Olrongai Congregations, all others were landless. Many of them depended on farming in portions of cleared forest areas. Worse still, those members of Rongai and Kampi ya Moto lived in very dry areas where they had more crop failures than harvests. Thus, this parish was so impoverished, so much so that no minister would have liked to go there. In fact, prior to my name being seconded to go there, another minister, Rev. Gatuku, had been posted, but he offered all kinds of excuses relating to his family, and when the appointment committee somehow got satisfied, my name was then floated and picked.

The dilemma was that where a parish had not cleared the cess for the previous quarter, the new minister would be paid only for the first three months. It meant that, no salary would be paid to the minister after that. As indicated above, Rongai was not struggling with the previous quarter but with an accumulation cess payment over a couple of years. This kind of situation then put me in a precarious position because I had kids whose schooling expenses were to be met. Looking back to my history and how God had always intervened in such awkward situations in my life, I, therefore, never negotiated against being posted to Rongai. I accepted the posting even as I put my trust in God, for my service was to the call rather than material gains. I anchored my faith in the words of Isaiah 41: 10-11

AFRICANIZATION OF THE CHURCH

One reason why I felt the need to push the Church to sing with action-accompanied songs was to liberate it from the enslavement of the motionless Scottish culture while singing to the Lord. Hence my choice of singing in an African style through a composition from '*Pilgrim's Progress,*' a school set book then. In doing this, I motivated the church to rebel from the stagnant Scottish posture during worship. I strongly believe in the Africanization of the Church. I believe that there are many aspects of the African cultural set-up that could be used to make Christianity appetizing. I believed in the application of rhythmical movements while singing, unlike the static missionary style. I also believe that there are many African musical instruments that can be used in praising the Lord. Unfortunately, the missionaries had labeled everything African as pagan. My aim was to engage the Church into borrowing some of the African musical ingredients.

I felt that,

> *"The PCEA style of worship should be modeled in the African context of worship. In giving us the Gospel, the Scottish Missionaries had also wrapped in Scottish cultural aspects. These hamper delivery of the Gospel in PCEA and other Missionary oriented Churches and hence fail to appeal and reach out to more and more young people."*

I further said,

> *"Africans have to adjust their style and mode of singing, in contrast to the Scottish static position. Incidentally, before the*

coming of missionaries, Africans clapped their hands, raised them up, jumped and applied all kinds of physical movements in worship. This was something that was demonized by the missionaries as a way of colonizing the minds of the African converts. They labeled these acts as pagan and ungodly. No wonder in Kenya, there are some Churches in whose Sunday services one has to strain to tell whether the service is a funeral, a wedding service or a Sunday service because of the general mood and atmosphere prevailing."

As if this was not enough, I further emphasized this message, driving it home by saying:

"It is high time we move to the new century (21st Century) with a renewed spirit of worship, for we worship a living God full of mobility. It is for this reason that the 21st Century should witness the fulfillment of Christ's word that says, 'Yet a time is coming and has now come when the true worshipers will worship the Father in spirit and in truth, for they are the kind of worshipers the Father seeks. God is spirit and his worshipers must worship in spirit and in truth' (John 4:23-24).'"

I concurred with Robert A. Raines who, in his book, 'New Life in the Church,' talks about the old and rigid order of the Church. In this regard, Robert says,

"The order is becoming so stiff and conditioned: so much that there is no room for new life."

To substantiate my point, I used to quote Bruce L. Shelley from his book, 'Church History,' in Plain Language in which he says,

"The church is often in danger of identifying the gospel with some cultural form in which the faith has found a home. And thus, missionaries failed to adopt to the ways of other people. They felt constrained to insist upon the expression of the faith in familiar ways' (pp. 293).

I likened PCEA Church to the life of a tree bearing bountiful fruits. Here, the fruits were a representation of the General Assembly, the branches were the Presbyteries, the trunk represented the parishes or parish sessions, and the taproot was the congregation. These are the visible parts of the tree. In the ground are four types of roots, which include tap root, which represents congregation. Then there are what I call primary roots that represent Elder Districts, then the secondary roots that I call Deacon Zones and finally, the hair root, which I likened to the members.

No wonder, then, I based the theme of the 17th General Assembly on the Gospel according to St. Luke 13: 6-9, in which Jesus gave a parable of a person whose responsibility was to care for the fig tree. Unfortunately, this person neglected the tree, and for three years, it yielded nothing. The owner of the tree furiously told the gardener to cut it down. This was because it was of no use and not productive. But the gardener pleaded, "*Sir …. Leave it alone for one year, and I will dig around it and fertilize it.*" In the same way, I felt the Church had been neglected and was not receiving the spiritual nourishment it deserved. This was just as the tree's rooting system lacked the necessary care and nutrients to make it fruitful. I therefore felt the spiritual desire to create ways for the Church to be spiritually fruitful. I also knew that I could only achieve this through Elder Districts. I, therefore, resisted any opposition or obstacles that could derail this process whose time for action had come. My strength was anchored in the words of Jeremiah 1:19; *"They will fight against you, but they will not prevail against you, for I am with you, says the Lord, to deliver you."*

MINISTRY AT RONGAI PARISH

Having laboured in Nakuru Parish for one year, I was transferred to Rongai Parish, where I reported there on January 7th 1986. This was one of those parishes that was part of Nakuru Presbytery. Geographically, it formed its western arm, with 2/3rds of it being in a very remote area. It was, therefore, the poorest compared with other parishes. As stated earlier, it had so much lagged behind in its budgetary contribution and in its physical and spiritual development that before my entry, the Business Committee had planned to have it dismantled. One portion was to go to the adjacent Njoro parish, while another to Nakuru parish and the third part was to go to Molo Parish. But the head-office decided to post me there first before this happened. They had known me as a hardworking person and a mobilizer when it came to the restoration of both the spiritual and physical perspectives of institutions.

One of the dilemmas that faced me was the wide dimension of this parish. Besides covering a big geographical area, it is comprised of 20 congregations. On the day of reporting, the parish session had met at PCEA St. Ninian's Church. I arrived there at around 9.00 am, though the meeting was to start at 10.00 am., I thought it wise to be around there earlier, just in case my help would be needed anywhere. After all, it would also be good to familiarize myself with elders, possibly knowing their names, their congregations and the distances from St. Ninian's. I also thought that as I shared with them prior to the session meeting, some would hint to me about the immediate needs in their congregations. When I reached St. Ninian's, I met about four elders who had already arrived. They seemed to be engaged in a provocative discussion. From afar, I could see them speak as they threw their hands in the air.

No sooner had they seen me than they stopped talking. I moved towards them with a big smile as I stretched my hand to them for a handshake. To my surprise, my hand remained suspended in the air for a while as if I was shaking the air before one of them very reluctantly stretched his hand and brought it into contact with mine lightly! As my hand got into his, I learnt through that contact that something was not right. This was further affirmed by the looks these people wore on their faces. When I looked at the next man, ready to shake his hand, he seemed reluctant to stretch his hand to me. And even when he finally shook my hand, he quickly released the grip as if he had touched a frozen metal. Their faces reflected anger and hatred. Nevertheless, I strove to extend my hand to the third person. He also shook my hand in a reluctant mood. The fourth one had his hands folded tightly, indicating that he was not ready to shake my hand. I really felt embarrassed and frustrated. I decided not to lose hope. I introduced myself as Rev. David Githii, the new minister. This was followed by a long silence, and then one of them said sarcastically, "*Oh, you are the new minister. How is that and yet we have Rev. Wahogo as our minister? Wahogo is here to stay?*"

I then realized that these people were treating me as an intruder. I then went and stood next to a nearby tree. I watched the elders as they kept coming in. I also noticed that these elders were standing in groups and each of these groups was engaged in talks. I could detect anger and bitterness in their talks and body language. I overheard one say,

"He cannot work here. We will, by all means, block him from serving our people. Remember, Rev. Wahogo defined him as a very inexperienced pastor."

More and more small groups had already continued to form in different parts of the Church compound, each being involved in what seemed to me as serious discussions. The four elders whom I first met had joined another group that was discussing under the roof of a building still under construction. While I was still under the tree, I turned my face to the road, where I seemed to enjoy the traffic. I then got into the Church, where the chairs were already arranged. It was an indication that it was the venue for the meeting. I got robed, getting ready to chair the meeting once it commenced. It was already getting to 11.00 am. Before long, the elders flowed into the Church. They were around forty of them. As they came in, none said 'hello' or smiled at me. The anger of the elders was portrayed by their red eyes, deep silence and their audible breathing. I had by now learnt that all was not well. I, therefore avoided the hymn singing and got straight into the Scriptures. Since the Christmas mood was still within, I read Mathew chapter 2:

1-12. I talked about the wise men and the way they got into Herod's palace to enquire about the possible birth place of the king. I said the wise men fell into error because rather than following the star, they opted to trust the earthly king. By doing this, they temporarily missed the Star of David. They looked down on man rather than looking up to the star that led them to the savior. I pointed out that, as we start working together let us be guided by the love of Christ. I told them that Christ emptied himself to come and die for the human race. I continued to say,

"Let us seek the wisdom from him, let us not deviate to seek the wisdom and the way to handle the parish from earthly people."

What I noticed is that the more I talked the more the elders' degree of anger heightened. This I could tell by the increasing rate of breathing and the way the eyes continued to expose their hatred for me. I discerned that the way they looked, not one word of what I was saying, was welcome. Finally, I concluded my devotion with a word of prayer. Whether they closed their eyes or not, I do not know! I did not dare open my eyes to look at them. Unlike them, my heart was full of Joy.

The more I looked at them as I expounded the word to them, the more my face shone with cheerfulness. I felt too much at peace. When I finished the devotion, I then asked, *"Any apologies?"* This question seemed to trigger the increased rate of breathing, and for the first time, I felt like my life was in danger. Unconsciously, I turned my eyes to where the exit door was, just in case someone would decide to give me one or two blows just to make me understand the seriousness of the matter. They were getting angrier because I seemed not to understand the depth of their anger; instead, I was constantly smiling and talking to them as friends rather than enemies. I proceeded to say,

"It seems we have no apologies; then could we take this opportunity to know one another since the agenda reads, Introduction?"

I paused and then continued,

"I already introduced myself in my devotional message, could we now start the introduction from the left going towards the right? You just say your name and the congregation you come from. I will know the rest as we interact in your congregations, homes and meetings."

Pointing to the person in the front row to my right, I said, *"Now, let us start with you?"* The breathing was at its maximum. The person who was supposed to start simply stared at me with what seemed to me a burning anger and hatred. His lips were making slight movements as if pushed by the emotions of anger. He stared at me until I said, *"Then, if my brother is not moved to talk, can we start from the left-hand side?"* The person stared at me and somehow wanted to burst out as the lips indicated, but he somewhat restrained himself from bursting out. I paused for quite some time and then said, *"Is there anybody who feels led to introduce herself or himself?"* Then, there followed a long silence that made the breathing so audible.

I now decided to make the next move. I said,

"I don't know you people apart from Mr. Gitahi and Kamunya, having seen them in the Presbytery meetings and even there, we have never engaged in any discussion. I have never seen any other person among you and I am sure likewise, apart from the two, none of the others had seen me before today. It has now occurred to me that you don't want me to be your minister; then let me advice you what people in your situation can do."

I paused, looked at them, lovingly then said,

"You should write to the Church appointment committee, express your gratitude to the committee for having thought so positively about your Parish and given you a new minister. Nevertheless, let them know that for some reasons which you will possibly give, you wish to be allowed to remain for some time with the old minister who still had some missions to accomplish in your parish. I am sure your plea will be listened to, and then I will be taken to another parish. I will always be given another parish. We have a great shortage of ministers, and that is why your parish has 20 congregations."

No sooner had I finished this statement than an elder from Kampi ya Moto congregation stood up and in great anguish, shouted,

"Write it yourself, write it! We have given you permission to write and say the elders have refused you to be their minister because they are not ready to part with their current minister. Write!"

I then realized that this was a psychological war that also needed some application of psychology. I knew I did not mean what I said because I would not do it anyway, but I said,

> *"You very well know that you are the ruling elders. I am just a moderator, and therefore, I should not restrain the decision of the session. So, if you unanimously pass that I write it, then I have no otherwise than to comply with your decision. For that reason, let me ask anybody who is opposed to that proposal given by my brother in Christ to state so now."*

I paused for some time, and as I stretched my hand reaching out for foolscap to write on, I said, *"Then, I hereby start writing what you as a session has authorized me to do."* I then bent down, pretending to start writing but in a very jovial mood. No sooner had I started writing than an elder stood up and said,

> *"My name is Philip Gitau, and I am an elder from PCEA Menengai. Before you write, I want to make a request for this session. Let us know the minister a bit. We would be defiant if the appointment committee got a letter from the pastor to whom we never even spoke a word. I am proposing that you stop writing the letter immediately. In any case, nobody seconded the proposal that you write the letter."*

Then I said,

> *"Yes, it's true the proposal was not seconded, but there is a saying that silence means consent. So, I took your silence to be an indication that you have all seconded the proposal. Anyway, it depends on what the session will say. I am such a flexible*

minister. If the session reverts to their former decision and opts for us to discuss a bit, then you are the ruling elders. I will just follow your instructions."

I knew that by showing them that they were better than me would be a catalyst to win them. I had heard a hint that the previous ministers were somewhat dictators. I, therefore, took the opportunity to let them see me as a totally different person, one who could do whatever the elder said. That was my secret. I now had my head up and then a hand shot at the back. I pointed to the person and said,

"Yes, brother, at the back, please remember to tell me who you are and where you have come from, and again, thank you for the Godly spirit to break the silence. Thank you also for raising your hand. "

The elder said:

"My name is Karanja from Umoja. Mr. Minister, I thought that it is important to tell you that we have deliberated for a long time that we refuse to accept you for no apparent reason apart from the fact that you are too green in the ministry. From some reliable sources, we have come to know that this is your first Parish. You were ordained a year ago, and for the whole of last year, you were under other ministers in Nakuru Parish. Our fear is that our Parish is really difficult to handle. We had had some senior ministers who have failed to create life in it - so we fear that with a green minister like you, our Parish is going to collapse in your hands."

As he sat down, three more hands were in the air. I now realized that my battle was halfway won because I was now controlling the session. Nobody wanted to talk without my permission. The tension was quickly eroding away. I could tell this by the reduced rate of breathing and the joy infiltrating their faces. I again pointed to a lady elder who said,

"Thank you, Mr. Minister. God works with blunt tools to shame the sharp ones; I am proposing that we accept this new minister. I am especially moved by his willingness to listen and abide by the elder's decisions. As he also puts it, I believe that he is flexible. This means, unlike some other ministers I have seen in this parish, he is willing to work with us. Also, as the book of Esther puts it, who knows whether he has come to our parish for a time like this? Again, what if his coming here is under God's plan? Doesn't God in Isaiah 46: 10-11 say, "My purpose will stand, and I will do all that I please.....What I have said, that I will bring about; what I have planned, that will I do. I believe that God has a purpose in bringing him here."

A fourth person whom I gave to speak sounded a bit negative, for he said,

"I am not sure that we are now making a good move. I have lived in this parish for many years. I don't see how an inexperienced pastor will unhurdle the hurdles we have in this parish. I don't remember any time we enjoyed preaching in this Parish because our sermons are constantly based on asking people to give money to pay our cess. It is my feeling that by

accepting this new minister, we are plunging our parish into a more precarious situation."

As the elders sat down, I ignored the many raised hands and said:

"I am really moved by the way you are carrying out your deliberations. From the few people who have spoken, I have already qualified each one of you as a mature person. It is now, with that confidence in your spiritual maturity, that I beg to ask you for a request. We all have a right to make a request to one he/she loves. You, too, can make a request to me. I am now requesting you allow me to be your minister for three months. We will not have another Kirk session meeting until the end of the three months (I was again playing it psychologically), after which we will come and revisit this issue. Again, I need to hear your feelings on this and let me say that I really appreciate the healthy atmosphere that you have now created."

Now, almost everyone had their hand up. I said, *"This time, I will only give a chance to the person who objects to my request."* One more person raised her hand up and said: *"Minister, we have come to a consensus. Reading the mood of the members of this Kirk session, we have accepted your request."* Her speech was intercepted by heavy clapping as a sign of agreement. Also, amazingly, almost everyone was smiling. I motioned the assembly to observe silence, and then I said,

"It is on that note that we will close our meeting. I will give out the program for the preaching and until it is out, could the chairmen of the congregations delegate the preaching to some

lay people at least for the next two Sundays? Meanwhile, I will be preaching at PCEA Kiamunyi next Sunday and at Menengai the following Sunday. Please, when we meet, say hi to me. We are co-workers in the Lord's vineyard."

I then pointed to a person to close with a word of prayer.

3. ESTABLISHMENT OF ELDER DISTRICTS AT RONGAI PARISH

MEETING ALL ELDERS

My first duty in Rongai Parish was to establish elder districts. I made a program of meeting all elders in their home congregations, as not many of the elders worked out of their locations. I organized most of these meetings to take place during weekends especially Saturdays. After the service, on Sunday, when I visited a congregation, I would also take time with its elders and deacons. They would negotiate on the boundaries of their Elder Districts. I would also educate them on how to carry on mid-week fellowships, the way to make visitations to the members' homes, the way to show love and concern to the needy and, of more importance, how to talk to the members not as bosses but as people using the towel to wash their members' feet. Their tongues were to be dressed in love as they talked to the members. In these elders' congregational seminars, I instilled a new leaning in their approach to their work. I also trained them on how to carry out Bible studies how to train members to be able to express themselves in Biblical terms, and even the ability to lead in the fellowships and in conducting prayers.

ENGAGEMENTS AND VISITATION

I engaged myself in joining the elders and deacons of various elder districts and in visiting the members. I used to be in the district sometimes as early as 8.00 am. I remember one woman from PCEA Menengai in whose house we got at 8.00 am. This woman showed a lot of reluctance in having us in her home. After sharing the Word of God, which was followed by praying and singing, she accepted Jesus Christ to be her Lord and savior. It was as she shed tears that she revealed to us how she had cursed us, and especially the pastor, for coming so early to her home, and then she said,

"Now Christ has opened the door of my heart, and in a like manner, the door of my house is opened. Come as early as you want and leave as late as you want."

This was just one instance, but each visitation brought many people to the Lord. The elders' and deacons' visitations, the showing of their love and concern and the midweek fellowships brought many people to the Lord, and many others who formerly never attended the Church became Church goers. This included especially the men, many of whose wives and children attended the Church but who opted to get lost in the world. Many, as a result of the Word, gave up their beer-drinking sprees and concentrated on the development of their families.

By the end of the second month, every elder I met wanted to dissociate himself/herself from the January 7th session meeting experience. They were also asking me to call a session meeting. All of them wanted me to understand that they had acted foolishly and it was as a result of being misguided by the former pastor and one or two elders. Each one of them asked for forgiveness from me for having resisted having me ushered into the parish. One recounted to me how I had been compared to vegetables in their early stages in a seedbed before later being transferred from the seedbed to the garden. These need to be watered before the roots mature to suck water from the soil and make food. So, the story went that I was like this vegetable plant being transferred from the seed bed to the Rongai Parish garden. The elders were to water me rather than myself watering the garden. I was not a mature minister and was, therefore, under all circumstances, to be rejected. As he put it,

"This was the reason for the resistance you encountered on January 7th. You were portrayed to us as an immature and a very inexperienced pastor. We have now realized that you are far much mature than our expectation. God has brought you here with a purpose. In just two months, the giving in our congregations has started to go up. There is a real revival building up. The district fellowships are helping to equip our members, and many are now getting excited about participation in both the fellowships and the Sunday services. It is so unfortunate that we had failed to follow the star and opted to seek advice from Herod."

In order to satisfy the desire of the elders, I then arranged for a Kirk session meeting in mid-march. All elders turned up. Each had a lit-up face. It was all smiles. Unlike the

January 7th Kirk session meeting, this time round, each one of them wanted to shake my hand. There were no pronounced groupings, and those who talked in groups of two or three talked calmly, and their talks were interjected with laughter. I called the session to order and then started the devotion in which I read Philippines 3: 1-12. I reminded the session of the importance of pressing forward, aiming at our goal, which in this case was the uplifting of the parish both spiritually and physically. In doing this, I explained we have all to forget the past failures and, at the same time, be willing to accommodate some changes. I pointed out that most of the PCEA parishes and presbyteries have continually lagged behind because they fear making changes. Some live to the point of having a cult that they worship called, 'Church Traditions.' Jesus had talked of the traditions of elders. The Pharisees' (elders) emphasized so much on traditions to the extent of neglecting all that would have glorified God. They constantly blamed Jesus for doing good on the Sabbath, including healing a person who had been sick for 38 years. I encouraged them to wholeheartedly and in one accord embrace the functioning of the Elders' Districts and the incorporation of the Holy Spirit in the worship, and before long, they would reap the fruit therein.

Having been done with the devotion, I then asked for an apology and there was none. I then said,

"This is our first session meeting. The last time we met, we finished prematurely, and no minutes were taken. However, we all agreed that when we meet next time, we would deliberate

*on whether you need me as your minister. Is this the issue you
still want to deliberate on?"*

The session clerk raised up his hand and said,
*"Mr. Moderator, from what I have heard from these elders,
they don't want this issue to surface. They want to forget the
past and press on for the good of this parish. They all have
confidence in you. In fact, if anything, they are very apologetic
about what took place the last time we met you as a session."*

Then, facing the elders, he asked, *"Don't you believe that?*
Then, there was a thunderous and a unanimous *"Yes!"*
I then said,
*"As I told you last time, I move with the ruling elders'
decisions. Let us then bury the hatchet and work on the
betterment of this parish both physically and spiritually. I have
really enjoyed the interaction I have in your midst in those two
months."*

When we came to the agenda, *'The parish we want,'* many
elders contributed to the deliberations- each giving very
well-refined thoughts/ideas. Then in one accord, it was
agreed that the highest priority be given to the promotion
of the Elder District management in the parish. Some said
they had already qualified it as the best way to reach the
members, where elders are even able to work one-on-one
with the members. As one put it,
*"The Church should have discovered this kind of ministry a
long time ago. I think we should point the accusing finger to
the pioneer missionaries who so much emphasized the*

corporate service rather than small group fellowships outside the Sunday Service."

We spent almost the whole session planning the methods to be applied to promote the spiritual and physical growth of both members and the physical development. The latter drew us to talk more about how to raise funds, but we came to a conclusion when I said,

"It does not matter how beautifully you design the money manufacturing techniques in the parish. The best and most beautiful way is to reach people's hearts with the Word. Feed the parishioners with the eternal food and money will automatically flow from the members. This is what Haggai explains when, in 2:8, he says, 'The silver is mine and the gold is mine; declares the Lord Almighty."

God also declares through Job that,

"I know that you can do all things; no plan of yours can be thwarted" (Job 42: 2)."

In emphasizing this point, I told them of a shepherd that I had employed at Mukungugu-Njoro. I did not know his name, but he called himself 'Halleluyah.' When this man came looking for a job, he described himself as a person devoted to his work, a person with long experience. The way he talked, I could not doubt him, and so I gave him the job. He had worked for about two months when I noticed that the cows were becoming thinner. When I questioned about the drastic change in the cows, he explained how he was seeking green pastures for them in the forest and that he also did not understand why, but he would try another area of the forest. Not before long, one evening, he was busy milking the cow. As he did this, he was whistling and sounded like he was in a jovial mood.

I drew near to the milking shed, but to my surprise the cow being milked was standing with the head far from the trough. It was supposed to be busy eating. It was for this reason that I bought some special milk-producing food known as 'dairy meal.' The cow was to feed on this food so that it could have a higher yield of milk. 'Halleluyah' had deliberately refused to give the cow the food. I then moved closer to the cow, only to see that the trough had no indication that dairy meal had been put there a couple of days. As I stood there, I felt the smell of beer. 'Halleluyah' was drunk, really drunk. It looked like he did not know what he was doing. The following day, I was sharing that experience with another person who, amazingly, said,

"We all assume that you know how your cows are shepherded. Your shepherd just drives the cows to the edge of the forest, and he leaves for the alcohol-drinking spree in the village. He usually leaves the drinking place at 3.00 pm to go and trace the cows in the forest. I am almost sure that those cows are never taken even to drink water for some days."

That day and without any notice, I paid 'Halleluyah' his dues and sent him away. Now, I challenged the elders not to shepherd God's flock like 'Halleluyah.' I pointed to the fact that people are like cows. If not fed well in green pastures, taken to water drinking places and fed with a spiritual dairy meal, then the giving will be very low. It is somehow a give-and-take system – it is a two-way traffic. I reminded them of 1 Peter 5: 1-3, where Peter calls upon the elders to feed the flock, not as if they were being forced, but because they should regard it as one's duty and a special responsibility. That session, which ended up like a seminar, caused a revival not only among the elders but into the parish as well. From that moment, the elders became very dedicated to their work.

FUND-RAISING

As stated earlier, Rongai parish was so impoverished in every aspect, including in its spirituality and economic status. I called a Kirk session meeting purposely to deliberate on the models of raising funds in order to meet the accumulated funds assessed to the parish, which was running into several thousands of shillings. After much deliberation, it dawned on me that we were not going anywhere. We were hardly getting any breakthrough. It was then that God gave me a revelation that I shared with them. The parish was to be categorized into Those who resided not far from Nakuru Town, those who lived in farming areas, those who resided in rather dry areas and those who resided in forest areas. I then proposed that the Parish hold a fund-raising drive. The fund raising was to be conducted through the Elder Districts.

The Elder Districts were to individually contribute a certain amount of money, and where money was not available, the members were to contribute the commodities that were available in their local area. For example, for those residing in forests, each district was assigned to make different items. Such included hoes' handles, cooking sticks, firewood, vegetables, potatoes, maize, onions, peas, etc. For those dwelling in dry areas, we agreed that they look for chickens because chickens did well in those dry and warm places. They hatch many chicks, and many survive and grow quickly. Those from farming areas were to collect goats/sheep, hens, rabbits, etc. Those living not far from Nakuru Town were to give money since many of them were in the working class while others were business people and farmers. Such included: Kiamunyi, Menengai, St. Ninians and Rongai. Having served in Nakuru Parish which mainly comprised of working class and business people. I used my influence to invite them to the set day for the fund raising. I sent invitation cards to both individuals and the congregations. I also thought out the kind of things that will be available for buying. I also requested them to pass the same information to their friends. I knew that they would scramble for hens and animals like sheep/goats, vegetables, potatoes and other products. I moved from one congregant to the other and fellowshipped with them in the Elder Districts and congregations.

During these meetings, I encouraged and motivated them as I pointed to their individual potential areas according to their productivity. I also sent a word to many people in the surrounding areas. Some were in desperate need of firewood. They cooked with dry maize (corn) stalks. The people from the forests enjoyed the finest firewood from indigenous trees which was so easily assembled. Such areas included congregations like Sabatia, Ecagiri, Maji Mazuri, Ravine and Endarasha. Many of the surrounding people were farmers who were again in desperate need of hoe handles. They all used hoes in digging and weeding their crops. Some of these forest congregations were to bring these handles for such hoes. At least almost every person would want a cooking stick, wooden spoons, etc. The day set for the fundraising was the first Sunday of September 1986. On the first Sunday of September, all roads led to PCEA Menengai, which was the venue for the fundraising. People came from all directions, some having hired some transportation, others by personal vehicles. Many of the forest congregations used donkeys to transport their items to be sold in the fundraising. People bargained for every item. Some hens were bought for as high as 1,500 shillings. Firewood, which was split into small pieces, fetched a lot of money. So many people had turned up such that the items were seemingly fewer than the demand so much so that not even one item was sold at the price we had anticipated.

Every item is made at a triple or double price. Other people pledged some money towards the support of the parish. Many from Nakuru Town did it so willingly because they were already my friends, and they needed to support me in my work.

I remember people like Moses Muturi and his family, Gitonga Muhunyo and his family and others working so hard to make sure that the parish was out of debt. The surprising thing was that by the end of the day, we had raised enough money to pay all the outstanding arrears that had accumulated in the past years and, on top, paid the 112,000 shillings, which was the assessed money for that year, 1986. By then, this was a lot of money. Thus, within the first nine months that I was there, Rongai Parish had its

"Financial sins washed away." It had a new birthing. Not long after that, I met one of the General Assembly officials who, after congratulating me, said:

> *"You know Rongai Parish had been a thorn in the flesh in our denomination. We had now come to a point where we were contemplating erasing Rongai Parish so that one part could go to Molo, another part to Njoro and the other to Nakuru Parish. Thank you for saving the situation and the embarrassment we were getting through that parish. Possibly, you will need to teach us the secret because I hear that in every institution you go to, you become its liberator."*

He jovially continued,

> *"This is what I hear of your works even at the schools you had headed before you joined the Ministry. I can only conclude that God has a special anointing upon the work of your hands. Rongai Parish has not only been blessed financially; it has also as well witnessed tremendous growth in spirituality. I hope you will not mind if in future we happen to post you down IN ANOTHER down trodden parish or institution."*

In terms of the parishes that had recorded tremendous improvement that year Rongai Parish led the way in the whole denomination.

PCEA PASTORAL INSTITUTE STUDENTS

One avenue that I realized could propel the growth of the Elder District in the denomination was to initiate that knowledge among the theological students. I also realized that the students could be a great catalyst in the promotion of spirituality in my parish. And now that I was a part time lecturer at PCEA Pastoral Institute, I organized with them to be spending part of their holiday time in my parish. Thus, in doing this I was killing two birds with one stone. It was a method I was applying to introduce the students to the ministry of elder districts who, after their graduation, would go and propagate the same in their parishes over the years. At the same time, I knew that being well theologically founded as well as being spiritual students, as I knew them, coupled with my very good relationship with them, they were to advance my vision of Elder District into the entire denomination. This would not only greatly uplift spirituality, but increase physical development as well as giving. These students used to come to Rongai Parish for two weeks during the holidays. Before reporting, I could send them an 'appointment letter' which indicated the congregation and the Elder Districts one had been posted to. Each person owned a parish in the form of an Elder District.

These students did wonderful work in the parish. They later became wonderful promoters of the Elder District ministry in their various parishes in different capacities, such as parish ministers, presbytery moderators and chairs of various committees in the life of the Church. As their experience continued to gain momentum over the years, so did the rapid growth of the Elder District ministry. As I write this book, all the ministers and elders in the PCEA Church have aggressively embraced the Elder District ministry. Ask any member of PCEA Church, and he/she will tell you that PCEA Church has greatly benefitted from the Elder District Ministry and one would wonder how PCEA Church could have survived without this viable ministry. Otherwise, if it were not for this invention of Elder Districts, PCEA Church could have a very minimal population.

Elder Districts have become the heartbeat of the entire denomination. Every activity in the denomination is anchored upon it. It has championed the avenue of giving, spiritual growth, physical growth and the establishment of new congregations. It has also created a spirit of oneness and individual caring of members and grown the spirit of Evangelism. Through it, the spirit of praise in worship has been greatly enhanced. But remember that in the initial introduction as I pioneered the Elder Districts, it was by grace. I had almost been kicked out of the PCEA Church. I had been accused of dissecting the Church into *"Small Churches"* within a given congregation. All said and done, the Presbytery was satisfied with my work and therefore recommended that I be given a Parish by myself. In this case, the Appointment Committee posted me to Rongai Parish, which was adjacent to Dr Arthur Parish.

COHESIVENESS IN MINISTRY

Rongai parish had a heavy load of twenty congregations. But nevertheless, I used to teach at PCEA Pastoral Institute every Wednesday of the week. I would leave Nakuru town (where I resided) by matatu at 6.00 am to cover the 100 miles from Nakuru to the Institute. I would then teach the whole day so as to cover church history within that one day; otherwise, for a residential lecturer, the lessons would have been distributed throughout the week. The final session begun at 2.00 pm and would end past 4.00 pm. I would then board a bus or matatu that would arrive at Nakuru around 7.00 pm or sometimes 8.00 pm, depending on how soon I caught the bus after the end of the classes at the Pastoral Institute. The Ministry at Rongai Parish was very challenging.

I encountered great opposition and rejection right at the onset. The parish itself was quite broad and the roads were quite rough and with poor transportation. The elders noticed my struggles and came up with an idea and incorporated some of the financially able people from Dr Arthur parish to organize a fund raising to buy me a car. It had the registration number KDU 386. That was my first car ever to own. I had to learn to drive before I could really take control of the vehicle.

Until then, I had never sat on a steering wheel of a car. By obtaining the vehicle, I became more mobile and available.

On Sunday, I used to report to one congregation by 8.30 am, preach and serve the Holy Communion as well as carry-on other services like baptism (if any). I would also receive the new members and then drive to another congregation for the 10.30 am service, which took me to around 1.00 pm. I carried the same services as above. I would then move to another congregation who would have finished the service and would be waiting for me. Upon arrival, I would serve the Holy Communion, give a word, and, if need be, attend to other required services. This carried me up to around 3.30 pm. In some cases, I could pass through another congregation who might have finished their services, gone for lunch and come back to Church to wait for me to administer Holy Communion at around 5 pm.

One would wonder why on earth people have to go home after the Church service and walk back to the Church at 5.00 pm or wait for a minister after they had finished the service. It is especially difficult for people in Western countries to understand this, bearing in mind that their services would normally take one hour. Furthermore, most churches in the West are used to having a minister almost every Sunday. But in my case, one has to bear in mind that I was catering to 20 congregations, and only an ordained minister could administer some of the ecclesiastical services.

This is not a paradox to the rapidly growing Churches in Kenya/Africa. The growth rate of Churches by far outpaces the training of ministers. Yet, unlike some western countries where there is already a great shortage of people willing to go to the Church Ministry, in Kenya and in all denominations, there are very many young people who want to join the ministry - the dilemma is in getting funds to train them. Thus, out of, say, 60 qualified candidates, the Church could only train 12 per year. This is even more so in the Presbyterian Church of East Africa. Imagine this congregation waiting for the minister or coming back at 5.00 pm.

If I were to minister to each congregation per Sunday, I would come back there after 19 Sundays, which would mean after almost five months. Hence, if one failed to take Holy Communion, it also meant one had to wait for a number of Sundays besides the previous time one had waited. This also applied to baptisms and the admission of new members. But it is good to say that, at the writing of this book, things had tremendously changed in the church administration. I had unblocked the foreign traditions that hindered church development. In many other instances, I had to minister to some congregations at night (especially the congregations located in the forested area). I would arrive at 6.00 pm and be served supper, after which we would start the service at around 8.00 pm. We sang hymns, I preached, baptized, welcomed new members and served the Holy Communion. I could also carry on some teachings on the doctrinal issues or answer questions that the members had. In such circumstances, we usually slept at around 1.00 a.m. or 2.00 a.m. In a number of congregations, they did not have a bed for me. They would gather the dry grass, spread it in a heap like a bed, and spread a few sacks on it and a torn blanket on top of the sacks. They would then have another not-so-good blanket to cover myself with.

In the morning, I would be given a cup of tea. The congregation could hardly afford a loaf of bread. I particularly remember PCEA Ecagiri and Sabatia Churches for this deplorable state. Despite the fact that I may not have had enough rest nor taken a good shower, if any, I would proceed to other stations according to that day's schedule. The schedules would include other areas of attention like funerals, weddings, marriage counseling, Church seminars, comforting the bereaved, hospitals and school visitations. All these indicate that I had a lot of work, but the joy in service was more uplifted by the willingness of the people to hear the gospel. They loved singing, sharing personal testimonies and fellowship. I also had time for the youth. The parish youth were very active. Once in a while, I could join them for an evening kesha (overnight prayers). This involved hearing the Word as preached by different individuals, listening to personal testimonies, singing songs and long prayer sessions. In those overnight fellowships, these young men and women could share the experiences in their Christian journey which would encourage others to keep on fighting the good fight. At such times, I could also take the opportunity to encourage them on how to face challenges in life as Christians. I was really enjoying this ministry when, in November 1987, I received a letter from the appointment Committee indicating that I had been transferred to Loresho Parish located in the outcasts of Nairobi. It was a 15-minute drive from the city centre next to Kangemi market.

MINISTRY AT LORESHO PARISH

I reported to the Loresho Parish in January 1988. This was a great contrast to my previous station. Loresho community is comprised of very rich people. It was a community of the elite people. Many of them had attained first or second degrees. A couple of them had doctorate degrees. They had big and expensive homes, many of them with Securicor guards and big and heavy gates marked *'Beware of dogs.'* They all drove to the Church, and many of them owned very expensive vehicles.

This differed greatly from the majority of Rongai dwellers, many of whom lived from hand to mouth, and almost 98% of their houses had earthen floors (uncemented), and none had a flashing toilet. They all used pit latrines that were built some yards from their houses. The latter were made up of poor-quality timber or mud walls. None had a dining table or dining area. The roads around them were not tarmacked, and very few of them had good jobs apart from those who were teachers. The Loresho people had everything most people would dream of having. They knew no hunger or lack of clothes or bedding. They had piped water in their houses. The minister's manse was expensively furnished with 3 bedrooms, expensive sofa sets, carpet, refrigerator, gas cooker, electricity, and telephone with extensions to the bedrooms. There was a car garage with an automatic electric door. Everything was a shock to me. Loresho people all wore expensive clothes which were washed through dry cleaning machines. The parish vehicle was a good, sleek model compared to my old-fashioned car. Back home at Njoro, my house had an earth floor, we used a pit latrine, and water was drawn by my wife or kids from a far distance by means of jerry cans. There had been no cold or hot shower. While taking a shower, one used to put some warm water in a small open container for use. One then scooped the water from the container and splashed his/her body with it using a smooth cloth to clean out dirt from the body. In cooking, we used firewood. We did not have electricity, a TV or a telephone. We had never owned a refrigerator, and hardly could we afford an everyday loaf of bread.

Loresho Parish had another culture that dissociated it from other PCEA Church congregations. It was a branch of St. Andrew's Church in Nairobi. The latter was a Church that for many years was under the management of Scottish ministers who believed that they were observing Presbyterian traditions, but, in the real sense, the traditions were Scottish. As for the Loresho Church, the administration was totally westernized with a mixture of both Scottish and American cultures because it was managed by American Ministers, unlike St Andrews, where everything was focused on Scottish traditions.

Before my posting, the parish had previously been in the hands of two American ministers who had manned it, each for at least five years. Thus, the members of Loresho, having been reared in Scottish traditions at St Andrews and then falling in the hands of Americans, felt they were more European/American products, and they tried to practice these two traits of western cultures. These ministers shaped the Church to be a representative of Western culture, where the minister read a ten-minute sermon. The whole service lasted for one hour. They also discouraged any altar call and /or a language that sounded like one was claiming to have come to know the Lord in a certain frame of mind. They referred to this as being judgmental and bordering on a holier-than-thou attitude. They claimed that their Church was known as a community Church more than a Presbyterian-based Church. In this case, they did not welcome the Presbyterian terminologies, including 'Women's Guild.' They talked of 'Ladies' but not 'Women's Guild.' There was no youth group. Instead, they had developed a kids' group. The other thing that made these people so reluctant to welcome me was my lack of Westernized culture.

They would have wished to have a minister who could say such things as, *"When I was in America or Europe..."* Academically, they would have welcomed someone with at least a Master's Degree. They did not even recognize my Bachelor of Divinity Degree from St. Paul's United Theological College. But what broke Carmel's neck was when in introducing myself, I told them a little bit of my background, including the way I grew in poverty with lice, bedbugs and fleas sucking my blood. But the worse was when I narrated to them my ministry experience in Rongai Parish, how I used to sleep on a dry heap of grass, and the way I enjoyed their very poor diet. I told them,

"You are very blessed people compared with where I have come from, Rongai, Parish. You are already living in Canaan."

I praised them for the development God had enabled them to do. I talked of the wonderful manse and the multipurpose hall, the Nursery School and in summary, I said,

"God has really blessed you. I have hardly been in a house like the one you have for the minister. I have never been in a parish with a sleek car like yours, and of great importance is being in the service of so smartly dressed people."

For sure Loresho people were and are smart. As for me I don't think I had owned a suit or a commendable jacket. All my clothes were old and of poor quality. In the midst of them, I felt displaced no wonder most of these people were not ready to welcome me in their houses. They really hated my presence in their Church. The chairman of the congregation/Church Board of Management was Ole Nchalo. I remember a day I called him on the phone to request that an idea I had be part of the board meeting's agenda. When the telephone rang, he said *'Hello.'* I then said, *"Praise God, this is David Githii."* No sooner had I mentioned my name than, in vibrating anger, he angrily shouted at me,

"I am not interested in who you are. But who gave you my telephone number? You should never call me."

He banged the telephone. Nevertheless, I treasure some
good memories of Mrs. Wanjenga, who had love and
concern for my welfare. At one time, she gave me 500
shillings to help me travel to visit my family in Njoro. There
were other very welcoming members to me, like Mr./Mrs.
Njoka, Professor/Mrs. Muriithi, Mr./Mrs. Njau and Muhia.
On the day of the board meeting, I carried the Bible in order
to share in the devotion as that is the undisputable work of
the minister. To my surprise when the chairman called
members into attention in starting the meeting, he never
called for the opening devotion and prayers. Yet that was
the procedure for PCEA Church meetings. But instead, he
said,

"Ladies and gentlemen, we will go on with our meeting and I
now call upon the secretary to read the previous minutes."

At this juncture, I stood up and said,

"My understanding, Mr. Chairman, is that every Church-
oriented meeting has to start with a devotion, which is
concluded with a word of prayer."

The chairman angrily silenced me as he said,

"Mr. Minister, this congregation has its own traditions and
its ways of handling matters relating to meetings and the
spiritual lifestyle of our members. In that case, we have nothing
to learn from you. We are very busy people. Many of us have
not gone home yet. We have just come from our places of work
and we just came for the business. After all, we had had very
civilized pastors from America who taught us the mannerisms

of handling meetings. This kind of talk is a waste of time, and with that, could the secretary read the previous minutes."

Surprisingly, even as the meeting progressed, I was not given an opportunity to talk at any point in time. My continued raising of hands were fruitless. I now started wondering why on earth the Appointment Committee moved me from Rongai Parish where people so much honored me and brought me to these very wealthy people who were spiritually so dry. I felt myself cursing the colleagues who had congratulated me for being removed from the *"wilderness in Rongai"* to the land of Canaan in *"Loresho,"* a land flowing with milk and honey. I remembered the words in Proverbs 17: 1,

"Better a dry crust with peace and quiet than a houseful of feasting, with strife."

Life became very frustrating. It was not long before the second board meeting would take place. This time, I was determined to have the meeting opened with a word of devotion and prayer. I hid a small Bible in my pocket. The members had finally settled for the meeting when the chairman said,

"Welcome to this meeting, which I hope will take the shortest time possible. Could the secretary read us the previous minutes?"

I abruptly stood up, opened my small Bible and said,

"Mr. Chairman, with all honour, we cannot go this way unless this is not a Presbyterian Church, and I believe it is because it

is for that reason that I got posted here. Under no circumstances should a Presbyterian board or session meeting begin without devotion or even prayer. That is why, Mr. Chairman, I now read the Word of God from the Gospel according to St Matthew chapter six, verses nineteen to twenty. This is a message that calls upon Christians stating as follows, 'Do not store up for yourselves treasures on earth, where moths and vermin destroy, and where thieves break in and steal, but sore up treasure in heaven…'"

I shared the message for 10 minutes. In conclusion, I asked one of the elders to pray. He prayed and from the prayer, I could feel that he had really benefitted from what I said. I had a breakthrough in the meetings that followed. The chairman used to call me, requesting me to go on with the devotion. I could tell that many of them liked the idea. But it was not a total breakthrough in all ways. There was a persistent spirit among some board members and the congregation who felt that a person of my caliber should not occupy their house or drive the parish vehicle. My status was considered far too low for that.

At one time, I could no longer travel with the parish vehicle to my home in Njoro. It was emphasized that only parish-related errands were to be attended to by me in the parish vehicle. I, therefore, failed to go home a couple of times because I could not afford the bus fare. My family was still at Mukungugu in Njoro, 140 miles away. I was also accused of giving lengthy sermons that lasted from 20 to 30 minutes.

My emphasis on the importance of people being born again also became a bone of contention. My use of some symbolic demonstrations in my sermons were disliked, especially when I compared immature Christians to bright, infected maize and a mature Christian with good maize. I also invited more attacks by bringing in some poverty-stricken children from neighborhoods into the Church on some Sundays. I thought it could be taken as a good gesture, especially when I called upon the congregation to consider a ministry to reach out to needy children. This time, I was personally confronted for having made such kids step on the clean carpeted Church floor. These kids had no shoes and had not brushed their teeth. Some of these kids were from the Kangemi area. Professor Njoka used to help me transport them in his pick-up. Then, it was not a surprise when they wrote a complaint letter to the head office accusing them of posting such a primitive and backward 'so-called minister" to this parish. They had demanded my immediate transfer and replacement with "a civilized minister."

At first, I looked at Loresho Congregation very negatively, but as time went on, I came to realize that there were as well quite a number of mature people who deeply loved God. In fact, what they lacked was guidance. Making an assessment of my sermons and teaching, they came to realize that I was a minister with great potential and that the Church had not sent me there by mistake. Within three months, most of the church members had come to embrace me with a lot of love and concern. They became very concerned with my life and family. They also came to love their Church being referred to as part and parcel of the Presbyterian Church of East Africa. They opened rooms for the Church groups, including the Women's Guild. Through my teachings, they came to realize that it was the foundation on which their Church was laid that never gave them the eye-opener to what it really means to be a Christian. The church was well equipped with some machines, including duplicating and typing machines. I, therefore, used them to produce some spiritual educational materials and articles. These used to be supplied to every member on Sundays. It greatly helped them to be spiritually enlightened.

A Christian worth his/her salt should be a loving person and ready to accept any minister despite the difference in status, education, material and spiritual possessions. After all, all that we own here on earth is left here on earth. Our bodies are like ripe bananas. The outer cover is peeled off and thrown away to rot but that which was covered is eaten to save life. That edible part of the banana is likened to God's Spirit, and the outer cover that is thrown away is likened to the physical body, which finally rots into the soil. Through some series of preaching based on Deuteronomy chapter 8, the majority in the congregation accepted the fact that, after all, wealth is not the measuring rod for a well-lived life, it is not a god to be worshipped. Christ-centered life is the key to a better life. For the first time, we came up with the youth morning service, which hitherto had been resisted. As I write, I still have sweet memories of PCEA Loresho church, and they are always in my prayers. It was while I was busy shepherding the Loresho congregation that I happened to meet Rev. Mwangi Theuri, a PCEA church minister. I enquired from him the criteria followed in going for further studies for I needed to engage in my master's degree. Mwangi is one of those people who have a spirit willing to help. He will always want to promote someone to achieve higher levels of life. Theuri then gave me contacts of ten seminaries in America and advised me to write to them requesting sponsorship to do a Master's degree in Theology. All the universities /Seminaries I had written to responded in one way or another. Nevertheless, it is the University of Dubuque that responded positively. They promised to give me a full scholarship so long as I would manage to meet the cost of the return air ticket. I, therefore, informed the PCEA Loresho Board members, who then organized a farewell party. It included raising funds to support me and my family. In total, they raised Kshs.50,000/=. Mr. Ole Ncharo gave a very moving speech which was marked by a lot of praise for my work. He said,

"We will miss your services, but we are happy that you have this opportunity to further your education. We have given you this money with much love. When you go to America make sure you know the price of food before you order. In some places, the food is expensive and might cost more than the money you have in your pocket. So, check the price and check your pocket. It would be quite embarrassing if you order food and end up not having enough money. You will find many things different compared to our lifestyle. On behalf of the

members of the board and the congregation, please accept our apologies for having failed to show love and acceptance at the time of joining us as our minister. From the teachings and preachings we have heard from you, we feel so enriched, and we would love to have you reposted here. You have a strong anointing from God."

The minister who was to replace me was Dr. Jesse Kamau. I had come to know Jesse more when he was the principal at the PCEA Pastoral Institute. Those were the days I used to come all the way from Rongai Parish to teach at the Pastoral Institute. I had come to know him as a very understanding man, a person who really loved people and would do anything to help a colleague in need. I also had the privilege to teach his late wife as a tent maker at the Pastoral Institute. I, therefore, had great confidence in him as the person to further streamline Loresho congregation in all aspects, physical and spiritual. With joy, I bid farewell to the Loresho congregation, and I treasure the sweet memories of our interactions.

4.OVERSEAS STUDIES

PICKED FROM THE AIRPORT

The time for me to leave for further studies finally came. The most exciting thing for me was to find myself on a plane. My mind quickly went back to my childhood and how much I would never have dreamt of being in a plane. The memories continued to unwrap, and before long, I was asleep. We reached Amsterdam in the morning. I then had a connection, and after some 7 hours, we landed at President Kennedy Airport in America. Yet another connection and I finally landed at Cedar Rapids in the state of Iowa around 9.00 p.m. A student by the name of John had come to pick me up. He had a placard raised, and on it was written, "*David Githii, welcome to America.*" I went straight to him. He came to me with wide open arms, embraced me and said,

"*David, welcome. I am sure that was a long fight. Do you have an idea how long it has taken you?*"

I said, "*Well, I am not sure, but I can work it out by tomorrow.*" John grabbed my luggage and led me to his car, and before long, we were on our way. John kept asking questions regarding my life and the country I had come from. After about 30 minutes' drive, John tapped me on the thigh and, in a jovial mode, said,

"I am sure, David, you are hungry. We can stop somewhere and grab a hot dog or some French fries. Which one do you care for?" I felt some confusion running in my mind - yes, I had heard of people who eat frogs, crabs and dogs - now, what should I tell this man? I responded in a rather confused tone and said,

"In my country, we neither eat dogs nor flies." John said, *"Many Americans like the sea food including crabs and even frog legs. They are delicious and very nutritious foods."* He continued, *"By the Way, David, I hope you don't confuse our hot dog with real dog meat and even what I call French fries is not a representative of the insects we call flies. These are potatoes that have been peeled and then fried in some cooking oil."*

I then said, *"Thank you for that correction. What you call hot dogs, I know it as sausages and for the French fries, we have chips."*

I also said, *"For sure, I am hungry and I wouldn't care for chips and what you call hot dog."*

Then he responded, *"If you don't like hot dogs or French fries, the other handy food or take away food is hamburger."*

I had never heard of hamburgers, and I hesitated to say yes, just in case it was another kind of animal that my people would curse me if ever they heard that I ate it. What if it ends up being snails? By now, John was losing patience, and he said,

"You know what, David; we have already passed two McDonalds, and I am sorry it will be difficult for us to get a place to buy take away food after the next place where we are heading to now."

I had not heard of take away which to me sounded like another kind of food. Finally, John pulled to a place written restaurant. The restaurant did not immediately mean to be a place to eat. In Kenya, I was used to the term' *hotel*' or '*a kiosk.*' John asked me to come out, saying,

"David, come in and make your own choice. This is why I have avoided the drive-through."

Again, I couldn't understand what a drive-through was. I had no idea what it was. Inside, John pointed me to what he called a sandwich. Looking at it, I noticed that it had raw vegetables. I had never eaten raw vegetables.

In Kenya I had always eaten thoroughly cooked vegetables. It was the animals that feed on raw vegetables. He said, *"David, do you care for a Sandwich?"* I now noted that John's joy had tremendously decreased, and I knew that something was not going well, but whatever the case, I would not give up eating the meat of a dog or flies. John said, *"David, look there and tell me what interests you."* Then I asked John, *"Might these people have a chapati or some kind of ugali?"* John started sweating. I knew we had a total communication breakdown. None of us seemed to understand one another. I then noticed something that I would love to eat and then said, "*Let me have the potato chips.*" John asked, "*Which one is that?*" I pointed to it and then John laughed so loudly that all in the restaurant gazed at him. Even as he laughed, he said, "*David, as I explained to you, that is what we call 'French fries.' You call it potato chips?*"

Our communication was being distorted by that deep American accent – I was used to the roots of European English. John now realized that I had a big problem with the names and the look of the American foods - hence, he said,

"*David, let me show you some of our food. He pointed to a picture of round meat placed between two round pieces of bread and said this is what we call a hamburger. The meat you see in between is beef. Anyway, I will tell you more about our food tomorrow. Meanwhile, what do you want to drink?*" I said, "*I will take some water.*"

John then ordered a glass of water. I saw the waiter scooping what to me looked like stones and putting them into the water. John handed me the water. On touching the glass, it was so cold that I felt like my hands were frozen. I said, "*Oh no. In Kenya, we don't drink cold water. In fact, many of us prefer hot water.*" John then laughed, making me the focus of attention all around. Then John said to me, "*David, these are not stones. They are ice cubes that make the water very cold.*"

Addressing the onlookers, John said,

"I am sorry for the inconvenience I am causing, but my friend here comes from Kenya, and he doesn't know what a hot dog French fries is, and now he says they drink hot water."

All those in the restaurant then fell into laughter but I did notice two or three faces that seemed to sympathize with me. Then John asked for tea, which was of great relief to me. We were again on the road.

On the way, I commented, *"This should be a special road. Since we started from Cedar Rapids, I haven't felt any sign of a pothole."* In reply, John said,

"Of course, having come from the African jungle, I am not surprised that you say this. I am sure your government cannot destroy the jungle - David, how do you live in the midst of all huge herds of lions, zebras, elephants, and rhinos, to name a few? What happens, for example, when you meet an elephant or a rhino?"

I now realized that this man had a very distorted image of Kenya as I had about what hot dogs and French fries stood for. He just naturally understands that lions and many other wild animals live with people. Why could he not understand that this wildlife lived in reserved areas known as national parks, such as Tsavo and Amboseli? As I was meditating on this, John went on to say,

"To me, this is one of the worst roads we have. I am sure in America; you will see wonders. You will visit malls like Wal-Mart and K-Mart. Many people refer to America as a 'land of

opportunities', and I agree with them. We have everything: all kinds of food, drinks, clothes, houses, and cold and hot showers. I am sure someone will give you what Americans call 'a house tour'. You will be amazed to see how much we are spoilt."

I then got muddled again and said to John,
"I think your use of English in some areas differs from the British English. An English person would say that Americans are blessed because the word spoilt has a negative connotation."

John picked on this and went on to tell me how the Americans, in their materialistic world, do not seem to put God at the center of all that happens in the human cycle of life. A big percentage of the American population has nothing to do with the God we preach. They have other gods, including the god of individualism, the god of materialism, the god of pride, and different gods for different programs, including sports like baseball, football and basketball. John went on to tell me that I would be surprised to see how Americans respond to the Church life. As he put it,
"Many of those who go to Church do it as a part of recreation. They want a sermon of ten minutes and a service of no more than one hour. As he elaborated on this, I could then see why Loresho Church had acquired the westernized culture in their order of service."
John continued to say,
"But this does not mean that all people in the churches are superficial Christians. There are thousands who love God with

all their hearts, only that their number is far much less in regard to Americans with over 300 million people."

LIFE AT DUBUQUE UNIVERSITY

At last, we arrived at the University of Dubuque. I was led to my room in Severance Hall, taken for a dormitory tour and then John left. I took a shower and then deeply fell asleep. John knocked at my door around 7.00 a.m. He alerted me that it was time to wake up and get ready for breakfast. He came again at 7.30 a.m., found me ready, and took me to the cafeteria. Here, there were hundreds of students. John introduced me to the profile of choosing the items I needed for breakfast. I marveled at the many choices of juices, types of bread and things like oatmeal, eggs, sausages, pancakes etc.

After some dietary culture shock, I managed to get enough to eat. John, at one time, silenced the students and took the opportunity to introduce me. As he concluded, he said, *"David tells me that he drinks warm or hot water rather than cold water, so do not expose him to ice water."* This was followed by a long laughter......

John went on, *"David also thinks we slaughter dogs and boil them, and then we have hotdogs."*

Another prolonged laughter.... *"Furthermore,"* he went on, *"David thinks that we breed much flies out of which we make French fries,"* another long laughter...

After breakfast, John took me around the university to introduce me to the dean, who, after some visits (as Americans would put it), took me to Rev. Carlos, who was the officer in charge of admission. It was Carlos who had so much corresponded with me on the process of admission. He is the person who ended up being a good friend including his wife, Paula. Carlos took me around, introducing me to the members of the faculty staff and the student leaders. He also led me in the process of choosing the classes for that semester.

Soon, I was alone in life, for everybody seemed to be very busy with deadlines of various assignments, set books to read, attendance of classes and class presentations. I also got plugged into the same hectic lifestyle. One Sunday, a student who had come from Alaska was assigned to take me to preach in a Church located in a place known as Cascade in Iowa. He was to drive me there. On the way back to school, he asked me,

"Now David tells me, I find you so smartly dressed in our clothes; I mean coats, jackets and pants (meaning trousers). What happened to your African clothes? I am made to understand that you people live in the jungle with animals and live almost naked, apart from some kind of animal skins that men and women use to hide their nakedness. I even hear that men are not, to a certain extent, mindful of covering up their nakedness. That's why I am wondering what happened to your African clothes."

I decided to make a joke about this. I replied;

"You know, no sooner had I landed at Cedar Rapids airport than I changed into American clothes. It is in the same way that upon my departure from the USA, I will take off the American clothes and then dress in my African clothes."

He then said,

"Okay. I now understand, but I also sympathize with you in that after enjoying our western clothes, you will then put them off. But I also understand that such clothes cannot remain clean and in good condition in the jungle bushes."

For the rest of the journey, I took time to explain to this innocent American that it is those who visit Africa as tourists, especially Kenya and Tanzania, who distort the image of Africa. Their main interest is to go on Safaris. In the national parks, they take pictures of wildlife and also pictures of some nomadic tribes who also live not far from this wildlife reserved areas.

For some reason, they don't see the need to take photos of Africans or with those who dress in Western clothes nor pictures of the tall buildings in Nairobi city with its heavy traffic jams. Why take a picture of the Hilton Hotel, and you have the same here? Why take pictures of the University of Nairobi, Kenyatta National Hospital, and the Nyayo Stadium while all such buildings are available in America? They instead focus on what is not commonly available in America, and in this case, they prefer the huge numbers of wild animals and the funny-looking and dressed nomadic people. People who live within these surroundings and whose life is characteristic or is dictated by the environment. As we got out of the car at the school, he was convinced that it is the people who visit Africa who fail to give both negative and positive aspects of Africa. He also blamed the African filmmakers who are so fond of showing movies of wildlife in Kenya as a way to promote tourism and failed to show the other side of the coin.

This man became my good disciple. He spread the positive side of Kenya. I also took the opportunity (now that I had known) to let the students get the true picture of our lives. I talked about our big city of Nairobi, with almost 2 million people and with some skyscrapers, paved roads, universities, and big Churches, and the fact that Kenyan Churches were among the fastest-growing Churches in the world. I had forums to explain how ministers in Kenya were manning a large number of different congregations and how the lay people manage the congregation in the absence of the minister.

My life at the University of Dubuque was embraced with love and concern from both the faculty and the students. Among the faculty members, I had good friends like Carlos, Linda Smith, Wallace (my Hebrew teacher) and Shannon. Among the students, I developed a lasting friendship with Dave Aldridge, Richard King, John Zeeman and Roland. The University of Dubuque remains so dear to me. It opened my horizon not only in the academic world but also in the American life. It helped me reach many people as I was assigned to talk or preach in various congregations. It was through this kind of contact that I came to have a very dear friend known as Rev. Chet Opkoski. Chet was by then a minister in the First Presbyterian Church in Lodi, Iowa. This was a Church I had visited several times in the course of my studies at Dubuque. The last time I visited the Church was on May 5th 2002, when the Church celebrated its 150th anniversary since it was founded. It was while in Dubuque that I met Dr. Robert Lorson who was a minister at the Westminster Presbyterian Church in Cedar Rapids. Robert invited me to preach in his Church. I also used to visit his home. Robert was a member of the Board of the University of Dubuque. He had served the Westminster Church in Cedar Rapids and then as an interim minister in First Presbyterian Church, Lancaster, Pennsylvania, Indiana Church in Pennsylvania and Tabernacle Church in Indianapolis, Indiana.

In my studies, I used to take some other religious courses at Wartburg Theological Seminary, which was about 3 miles from UD. I would have encountered a lot of problems as I walked there due to snow, but thanks to Rev. Richard King, who volunteered himself to give me a ride. The going was, at times tough due to the snow covering the road. Surprisingly, I had not seen snow before. But then, there was this day in late November. I was in my room and looking outside through the window. I noticed small, whitish, cotton-like things falling from above. I thought it was some kind of substance falling from the trees, but these things continued to fall.

After some time, to my surprise, the ground had turned white. I went to the person next to my room and enquired what that whitish substance falling everywhere outside our dorm was and why even the ground had turned white. He told me,
"*David, that is snow falling. We are already in winter. That is why we have a saying, 'Make hay while the sun shines.'*"

He went on to tell me that, henceforth, we will be enjoying less and less sunlight. My friend expressed surprise that I had not seen snow.

In this connection, he said, "*David, don't you have winters and summers in your country?*" I then started a long conversation with him. Everything I said to him was also a surprise. I told him that Kenya is transversed by the equator, and it is hard for us to experience winters. I also touched on issues like the fact that we don't have long summer holidays as they did. Our schools run on a quarterly basis, running from January to the end of March, May to the end of July and September to December. This means the months of April, August, and December are holidays and no schools are in progress by then. I also told him that the only place where snow exists in Kenya is on top of Mount Kenya, which is 17,000 feet above sea level.

As my studies drew to an end, some members of the faculty, mainly Linda and Carlos found it necessary that I take a Doctor of Ministry Degree.

All arrangements were made, and a congregation in which I could be living as I continued with my studies was identified. The plan was also to work out how I would have my family brought to the USA. When everything was well planned, a letter was written to my Church in Kenya explaining the willingness of the University of Dubuque to sponsor my doctoral studies. Unfortunately, the PCEA secretary General found it inappropriate for me to engage in a doctoral program. At the time, no specific reason was given for this decision. However, I assumed that there was fear that my further advancement in education would make me a potential candidate for the moderator of the General Assembly seat. Someone in the office did not want to open such a door where I would be a competitor. I was, therefore, recalled home. Thus, immediately after my graduation on May 15th 1989, I flew back to Kenya. I was appointed for full time teaching at PCEA Pastoral Institute. But it turned out to be a frame time of six months.

THE STRUGGLE IN RAISING MONEY

After leaving Dubuque and having lost the opportunity to do the doctorate of Ministry degree, I decided not to give up. There was a burning desire in me to do the final lap in the academic achievement. I was even more concerned because the PCEA Church had hinted at commencing a program to start a university for the Church. I felt that I should prepare myself for this kind of responsibility, to teach in this upcoming Presbyterian University. I, therefore, contacted both Linda Smith and Shannon, who were my former teachers at Dubuque. They then contacted Fuller Theological School in Pasadena, California. Shannon even paid for the application fee. I proceeded with the application procedures. The handicap came when I had to show the availability of $12,000 towards the accommodation, insurance and tuition fee. The letter had categorically stated that in no way would I receive an admission letter 1-20 sent to me until I showed availability of this money.

I did not have the slightest idea of how to obtain the money. Just then, I came across the book by Robert Schuler on Positive Thinking. I read this book not once but three times. This keen reading turned my mind positive. I could not see defeat; my mind had become so energized. In the book, I learnt how Robert moved to California to start a Church with only USA $500. His first congregation had three members, including himself, his wife and their daughter.

Due to the power of positive thinking accompanied by prayers, Schuler, in later years, had one of the biggest Churches in the USA, a huge sanctuary that filled with thousands of people every Sunday. This is the Crystal Cathedral in Anaheim, California. In my current challenge, I therefore decided to be more positive that all would be well. I also got hooked into another prayerful gear.

Relentless Life Bumps

TOM KIRKPATRICK

First, I wrote to a minister friend, Tom Kirkpatrick. He was the minister of the First Presbyterian Church in Galena. I had come to know Tom through his wife who was taking a Hebrew class with me at Dubuque. One day, we sat next to each other and I had a chance to answer many of her questions relating to Kenya. I then remember her saying,

"I am sure my husband would love to have you speak to his congregation. It is important for them to hear you talk about the Kenyan Church and how they are vibrant in their worship services, participation in the Church and the depth of their faith."

Later, Tom invited me to preach and speak in his Church. I preached in the morning service. I remember teaching from Deuteronomy 8: 1-21. This is where Joshua reminded the Israelites not to forget their God when they got into Canaan which was a land flowing with milk and honey. I therefore reminded the congregation that comparing themselves with people like us in Kenya, and as they lived in a land of opportunity, a land with almost everything at hand, they should not have another god of materialism. They should not think they have accomplished all that they have through their involvement in the busy schedules, and the technological achievements, but through God who made it so for them. They had all they needed within and all around them. After the service, there was what is known as a potluck. This is the time people come together, eat and sometimes have a speaker. In this potluck, I was the speaker. I again took the opportunity to explain to them the rapid growth of the Church in my country and the poverty in Kenya, resulting in poor medical and educational facilities. I also talked about the inadequacy of both theological and secular learning institutions about the thoughts of the PCEA to come up with a university that would accommodate these areas in higher learning.

I gave them an example where the highest theological degree one could attain from the protestants was the Bachelor of Divinity at St. Paul's United Theological College. It was also for the same reason that I had come to take a master's degree in America. It was with this background that I wrote to Tom, explaining my desire to further my education in preparation for the upcoming PCEA University. The Galena Church is devoted to giving $5000 to Fuller Theological Seminary towards my education if I finally get admitted there. This left me with a balance of $7000. It was proving difficult, but then I took courage and upheld the power of positive thinking, which cannot happen unless it is submerged in purpose, trusting God and unswerving faith. Therefore, I prayed and prayed with a focus on God's Word in the book of Joshua 1: 9,

> *"Be strong and courageous. Do not be terrified; do not be discouraged, for the Lord your God will be with you wherever you go."*

THE FUNDS DRIVE AT DR. ARTHUR CHURCH

It was after much praying and upholding faith and at the same time thinking positively that an idea came to me, *"What if I mobilize my friends for a fund-raising drive?"*

This sounded like a good idea. I, therefore, went to the elders and minister of Dr. Arthur Church in Nakuru Town, who then so willingly gave me their Church as the venue to hold the fund-raising function. This was after I had given them my proposed date which was in the month of June. My dilemma was that being a teacher at the pastoral institute, I did not have easy access to a congregation; hence, I had to contact Dr. Arthur's Church elders and the minister. The other dilemma I had was that it had been a while since I was in Nakuru and it is said 'out of sight, out of mind.' The other dilemma was that the only day that was somehow available to use Dr. Arthur's sanctuary was also a day when the parish kids' Sunday school competitions were being held. Having no other alternative, I took the day after some consultations with Sunday school parish leaders who promised me that they would try their best to bring the competition to an end, latest 2.00 pm.

I then embarked on tracing my friends in Nakuru, which also became another dilemma because the pastoral institute was over 70 miles from Nakuru. The only time available for me was on weekends. Nevertheless, I tirelessly approached a number of friends, giving each a number of people they could approach on my behalf. The elders also helped me in announcing in the Churches. I also sent letters to other nearby parishes. Finally, the day for the parish competition, which was also the day for the fund-raising, came. The kids' competition never started until 11.00 a.m. It was said that some adjudicators never showed up on time. The other thing was that the adjudicators did not know me, and their minds were focused on *'a slow but sure attitude'* in their program. I also noticed that confusion among the Sunday school leaders arose around the area of feeding the kids and that some trophies had not yet been brought. No wonder they seemed to have more important issues to attend to, and my fund-raising became a secondary issue. There were around 20 groups to participate in the competition.

The competitions included a play, a folk song and a set piece from every group. The last two started and ended around 1.30 pm. This was followed by a lunch break and drama competition that started at 2:30 pm and went all the way to 4:30 pm. Then, followed the performance analysis and the issuing of trophies and certificates. Everything came to an end at 5:30 pm. My guests had started arriving on time, and by 2:30 pm, there was quite a crowd. But then, after 4.00 p.m., I noticed that the number was decreasing. They had become impatient as the competitions dragged on. But there were those who, before departure, would come and say something like,

"I had some guests at 4:00 pm, so you will excuse me, "or" I come from far, and I cannot wait anymore. It's unfortunate that the competition has taken so long."

A few such people handed their contributions to me. Others would come and say something like,
"I'm gone, but I will be coming back, but of course, they never came back."

Unfortunately, there were quite a number who went without giving me their donations. By 5.30 p.m., only a handful of people were hanging around. But the worst of all was that in the course of time, two of the three guests of honour were not in sight. It was around 6:00 p.m. when a handful of people settled for the fundraising. In total, we collected Kenyan money equivalent to $2000. This added to Galen Church's contribution which had given me a total of $7,000, leaving a balance of $5,000. The situation was proving an uphill task, but I kept on focusing on Joshua 1: 9 and also, Isaiah 41: 9-10,
"You are my servant; I have chosen you…So do not fear, for I am with you; do not be dismayed, for I am your God. I will strengthen you and help you. I will uphold you with my righteous right hand."

And with this strong will, I persisted in prayer. I had anchored all my hope on the fundraising. The Sunday school competitions had failed my day, but I also felt good because it was Jesus who said, *"Let the children come to me."*

I felt like hating the Sunday school leaders and the adjudicators for not galloping in the competitions, but then a spirit of forgiveness grabbed me, and I felt at peace and the need to love them. But also, the big question that remained with me was,

> *"What is the next step? Where do I move from here? What are the options?"*

The more I contemplated these questions, the more I sought ideas from my friends, and the more I felt at a loss. I then had another idea,

> *"What if I go through all the contacts that I had made while in Dubuque? Possibly, I might find a person I can address my problem to."*

DR. JOHN TOAY

As I perused over the addresses, I came across the personal card of Dr. John Toay. John was an alumnus of the University of Dubuque Theological Seminary and I had met him when he had come to give a speech in the school. After the speech, I took time with him, asking him questions relating to his speech. I also answered some questions he had asked me about Kenya. I remembered his final words to me as we parted company,

> *"I admire the depth of your faith, and God has bestowed upon you, the potential of leadership and also of a teacher/lecturer. Unfortunately, I have to leave you as I have to catch my flight back to California, and now that you have my business card, please keep in touch."*

John's address read California, and I therefore thought of writing him to inform him of my dilemma in getting tuition to enable me to get admission at Fuller School. I made this decision because of the fact that he resided in California, where Fuller School was located and also due to the positive attitude in which we had parted company while at Dubuque.

I, therefore, decided to write him. I wrote quite a lengthy letter that I sent him. I first reminded him of our meeting at Dubuque, after he had given the speech there. I told him how I appreciated his very positive impression of me. Then, I narrated my problem of raising $5000 to join Fuller for further studies and the importance of my studies in relation to teaching in our Presbyterian Theological Institution. I finally made an appeal for his support in this worthwhile project, which would well be interpreted as some mission work for his Church in a different part of the world.

THE PHOTOCOPY

A s I continued perusing over the contacts I had picked while at Dubuque, I came across a photocopied document with some Churches in California and their addresses. I made the copies after I came across the USA Directory of Presbyterian Churches. I was moved to do this after a day Linda Smith, who, after realizing that it had become impossible for me to study for a Doctorate of Ministry at Dubuque, had said,

> *"Possibly in the future, you could try Fuller Theological Seminary. They have a very good program in the School of World Mission which also gives some scholarships."*

So, when I saw the Church directory, I photocopied some pages that had some Presbyterian Churches around Los Angeles where Fuller Seminary was part of as it was located in Pasadena. I cannot figure out why I had to go through the struggle of doing this photocopying, but I had just done it.

Thus, in deciding which Churches I was to write to, I looked for Churches with a big capacity of membership. I wrote to seven Churches, including St. Andrews Presbyterian Church, located at Newport Beach. I again explained the fact that Fuller Theological Seminary had admitted me for further Studies, but they could not send the I-20 to me unless I indicated the availability of $12,000. I then made them understand that I had already raised some money and had a balance of $5000. I further explained the importance of furthering my education. I laid my hands on the letters and posted them. I received responses from some of the Churches I wrote to. But all answered with regrets. Only St. Andrew's Church gave a semi-positive answer. They thanked me for writing to them. But also expressed the fact that their Church was so committed to mission work, leaving them with no breathing space to come to my aid. Then Rev. Dr. Bill Flanagan, who wrote the letter, promised me that despite the impossibility of them to support me, they would keep me in their prayers. I wrote back to him, expressing my appreciation to him and the mission committee of their Church for taking time to deliberate on an issue from a person they did not know. I highly commended them for their Godly Spirit. I did not lose hope as I kept on waiting for any other belated responses from the Churches I had written to, including Dr. Toy. I kept on waiting.

It was by now the month of October. Yet, I was supposed to report at Fuller in January 1990. Day after day I kept on waiting and in persistent prayer. The waiting bred hopelessness, and by the beginning of November, my positive thinking was being eroded fast, but I kept on applying spiritual breaks to it. I knew the worst I could do was to get into total desperation. I prayed and visualized the success. I kept on somehow enticing my mind to see myself boarding a plane heading for California, USA. Whenever I missed sleep at night, I focused my mind on thinking positively and, at the same time, praying about the possibility of God coming in at the last minute. My hope was built on the various portions of the Scripture that I kept on reading that portrayed how God had come into people's lives at times of total despair. I read such portions like the time when Peter was put in prison. When he had been securely guarded and chained with doors made of strong and heavy iron, God sent an angel of the Lord to rescue him. From this text, I also learnt the importance of prayer as the key to unlocking the tightly locked doors, for the Bible says, *"So Peter was kept in prison, but the Church was earnestly praying to God for him."*

I was also reminded of the turmoil that the disciples faced in the lake, as recorded in Matthew 8: 23-27. Verses 25-27 states that,

> *"The disciples went and woke him, saying, "Lord save us!....Then he woke up and rebuked the winds and the waves, and it was completely calm."*

Yes, the storms were raging, and when they were almost losing hope, they remembered that Jesus was with them. When they alerted him of the storm problem, He commanded the strong winds to stop. That really stirred my faith, which then continued to help me uphold the grip upon my trust in God. I was also reminded of that time when the children of Israel were trapped between the Red Sea and the fast-approaching Pharaoh's army. The act of Moses stretching out his hand with a stick in its grip resulted in the sea parting, creating a big boulevard or a highway for the Israelites to pass through.

These memories encouraged me more by letting me know that God does not come to our aid in thunderstorms or big jets; He comes in simple ways that sometimes leave us amazed. This also happened to Abraham. His son Isaac had earlier questioned the availability of the sacrificial ram, but Abraham had responded by saying that *"God will provide."* And true to his words, as he was lifting up the sword to slaughter his son, Isaac, God's voice calmly stopped him, instead directing Abraham to a fat ram caught in the thicket. In the same tune, I kept on telling my heart that 'God will provide.'

THE BREAKTHROUGH

Even as I waited, wondering what my next step would be, I continued teaching at PCEA Pastoral Institute. One day after class, I went to the Institute mailbox, where, to my surprise, I found a letter from Fuller Theological Seminary.

Upon opening it, I found it had been written by Paul Pier's son, who had introduced himself as the dean of the School of World Mission at the Fuller Theological Seminar. In the letter, he congratulated me for being admitted to Fuller Theological College starting in January 1990. In a separate note, he had attached to I-20. The letter partially read...

"You know, David, having read all your correspondences to Fuller, all of which fell in my hands as a dean, I really felt that you are such a potential person to your Church, and I felt it my mission to at least help you come to Fuller. And now, welcome to Fuller. You will like it and May God be with you as you prepare for more productivity in God's Kingdom. And having read your CV, my discernment tells me that there is something divine in you, and God has given you great potentiality in the area of leadership."

It was upon this realization that I commissioned myself to fundraise for the required package of $12,000.

Now, with the $12,000 package being ready, I wrote to the PCEA Training and Personnel Development Committee requesting the committee to grant me leave to go for further studies. I knew this was not an easy bone to crack, but I felt that the Lord had to overcome the resistance as per his Word in Isaiah 9: 7, which says, *"The zeal of the Lord God Almighty will accomplish this."* I was more aware that some of the officials of GA would not easily allow me to go for further studies. It was not long since they had blocked me from taking the Doctorate Ministry at Dubuque. But I wrote to them anyway. My request was tabled before the Training and Development Committee where it was extensively debated upon. The spirit of resistance was very high as those for my proceeding for further studies stood their ground. Things were made more difficult because the General Secretary of the Church had influence over the Training Committee, and he was opposed to my going for further studies. Finally, the pro-group insisted that the matter be referred to the Business Committee. Such a matter had never been heard of. Matters to do with the Training Committee ended in this committee. Remember, the opposers were focusing on future Church leadership. Their opposing was a way of blocking me from becoming either the Secretary-General or the GA Moderator in the future. They discerned my leadership potential. Such training matters are never referred to the Business Committee, but this one was. Now that the SG was not the secretary to the Business Committee, I got enough support, which then opened the way for me to proceed with further studies.

The Church provided me with the air ticket and on 2nd January 1990, I took off from Jomo Kenyatta International Airport for California, USA.

TWO DAYS STOP OVER IN ATLANTA

Prior to my departure, I had gotten in touch with my good friend, Rev. Ngoima, who was doing his doctoral studies in Atlanta, Georgia, USA. I was to stop in Georgia and be his guest for two days. I arrived there on 3rd January and spent two days with him and his family. Our being together was marked by many discussions that went all the way to the time we got interviewed to join Holy Ministry. We talked about our life at St. Paul's United Theological College, as well as our ministry in the Church. We also talked about the big ideas that we had in order to promote and create a new spiritual move in the PCEA Church that we loved.

We also talked about the role we would play in the training of ministers. To us, this is the key to a better Church. Well-trained ministers pave the way for a well-cared Church, a growing Church, an ever-renewing and reforming Church, a well-rooted Church in its physical, spiritual and social life. We felt that God had given us an opportunity to go for further studies because he had a mission for us to accomplish in the Church. I also talked to him about my desire to see that the Elder Districts would be the base of the working system in our Church. I had always visualized a Church where all elders had their ministry concentrated and focused in the Church's small groups that he/she manned. I remember telling Ngoima,

"You know, I liken the members of the Church to the root hairs of a plant. These hair roots are quite minute and vulnerable,

but it is through their sucking of the mineral nutrients from the soil that determines the strength and fruitfulness of a tree."

I also remember explaining to him that as the health of the tree will be determined by the richness and the fertility of the soil from which the hair roots suck that fertility and pass it to the rest of the tree, so are the members of the Church (hair roots). It is the spiritual fertility that they suck in the Church's spiritual lifestyle that determines the spiritual and physical uprightness of a Church. This, as I explained to him, is achieved by reaching the members through small groups, in this case, Elder Districts. This would enable the Church to grow in strength and be fruitful in all its aspects, including financial giving. Rev. Ngoima thanked me very much for the courage I had in starting this movement. We also talked about the way I had the movement started at that initial stage of my ministry, even before I got ordained. I gave him my experiences at Thogoto Parish where they almost blocked me from being ordained by accusing me of bringing about subdivisions within the congregations. Further, I enlightened him of my endeavor to establish Elder Districts at Nakuru and Rongai Parishes. I remember Ngoima in response saying;

"I see you have a big dream in deepening the roots of both the spiritual and physical growth of PCEA Church. That is your original idea, and as you put it, if it permeates the whole Church, then I have a different visibility and mobility in our Church. I am aware of the opposition you have encountered, but this is a battle you have already won. Many of those elders and pastors who used to question this movement have already

calmed down. I just pray that those who have not fully accepted it will finally yield when they realize its benefits."

I stayed with Rev. Ngoima from 4th to 5th of January 1990. I also had the opportunity to see much of the state of Georgia and mostly the surroundings of Atlanta. On the 6th, he escorted me to the airport, and off I left.

5. THE BEGINNING OF A MIRACULOUS PATH

THE FLIGHT FROM ATLANTA TO FULLER SEMINARY

The plane I got in at Atlanta was not full, and it was destined to make two stops to pick up more passengers. We first landed at an airport in Alabama. Some people got in. A man almost sat next to me as the seat was vacant and, after a further study of his ticket, moved on - yet another one came and almost thought he had identified his seat as the same one but proceeded on realizing it wasn't. Before long, we took off and then made our second landing at Fort Worth International Airport in Dallas, Texas. More passengers got in, and a lady took the seat next to me. We kept on waiting for the fight to take off. It had taken rather longer than the time we had spent in the previous Airport in Alabama. The passengers' anxiety was building up when the pilot announced,

"Ladies and gentlemen, we are experiencing a small problem; a red light is appearing on one of our doors. We are working to put it off. Please bear with us; we will soon be in the air."

It was then that I turned to this lady who was sitting next to me. I decided to break the ice by saying to her, *"Hallo, my* name is David Githii from Kenya, East Africa." Then, a discussion developed that went like this:

The Lady: *Oh, hello, David, my name is Elise Alsop from Northampton, Massachusetts. I wonder, is this your first time to be in America?*

David: *Oh no, this is my second time. I was in Iowa not a long time ago, taking my Master's degree in Theology from the University of Dubuque.*

Elise: *How nice, so you have a Master's degree in Theology? In which field?*

David: *I obtained a Masters of Arts in Religions, Degree.*

Elise: *What other religions have you covered in that study?*

David: *This degree involves a lot of history as well, but on the religions, I have extensively covered Islam, Buddhism and Hinduism, among others*

Elise: *How do you judge all these other religions?*

David: *You know the final judgment is with God, but we Christians believe there is only one way to get to heaven. And I am inclined to that belief.*

Elise: *I am also a Christian, but the sweetest part of it is that I am born again. You said that not a long time ago, you were in America, what had you mostly missed in the course of your absence, having gone back to Kenya?*

David: *I had missed many things, but more than any other, I had missed pizza.*

Elise: With some excitement, she said, *"David you love pizza to that extent? That is exciting. I also love pizza but I also love other American foods, including tilapia fish.*

Just then, the pilot announced,

"We are sorry for the inconvenience earlier caused, but now get ready for departure. Soon, we are going to head for the takeoff terminal; we are through with the red light."

We were almost getting to the spot for the takeoff when the pilot said, *"Oh, this is very frustrating. The red light has shown up again. We have to go back and give it the final trial."* Thus, we went back, and as the plane stopped, the pilot said, *"We will work out this problem, but meanwhile, if you feel the need to stretch out, you can get out, but make sure you don't go far."*

Elise then said to me, *"Well, David, I will stretch my legs a bit."* She left me stuck in my seat. I was almost falling asleep when Elise awakened me. She touched my shoulder tenderly and said, *"David, here is the food you like, Pizza!"* To my surprise, the Pizza was beautifully wrapped. I stretched my hands and Elise so lovingly placed it on my hands. I said, *"Thank you, Elise, you are such a wonderful and generous person."*

Then Elise said:

"You know, David, God has made us to be wonderful people, especially to strangers. It makes me happy to meet a person of a culture totally different from mine, and someone I can communicate to. You know, we Americans have a very distorted worldview about people from Africa. I had hardly ever imagined a person from Kenya would be able to speak in English. What I have mostly seen are some tall people in Kenya, dressed awkwardly and living among wild animals.

You will be surprised, David, because immediately you said you come from Kenya. I quickly glazed in your face and arms to see any scars caused by the wild animals."

Then Elise further said, *"Sorry David, I should have left you alone to enjoy the warm Pizza."* The short silence that followed was broken by the pilot, who said,

"We are now sure that our problem of the red light is over; please take your seats, fasten your seat belts and be ready for the take-off." Soon, we were on the run-away and, within the next few minutes, were above the clouds.

As I enjoyed the Pizza, my mind was getting further excitement as I visualized landing at the Los Angeles Airport. As I alighted, I saw someone holding a placard reading 'Rev. David M. Githii.' Then, the person would drive me to Pasadena, where Fuller School was located. I longed to see Los Angeles and to be in the class taking notes as the lecturer taught us. I could visualize myself seated in the forest of books in the library. Elise, by this time, was temporarily asleep, possibly to give me time to eat the pizza. Soon, I was through, and I got into a meditative mood.

I looked at Elise's face and my mind then started working on her. I thought to myself, what a good example of a true Christian, one living in the real Christian lifestyle? How beautiful would the world be if all Christians were so much loving, caring for the needy and the strangers, giving the right spiritual guidance to the needy, just the same way she had fed me with what I needed: the pizza.

The saying is true, *"You will know them by their fruits"*, for actions speak louder than words. This kind of thinking had invaded my mind when the pilot announced,

> *"Ladies and gentlemen, we have cruised enough; it is now less than one hour to our destination, Ontario. Please, enjoy the rest of the fight."*

This announcement caught my mind like an electrical shock. The announcement had already awakened Elise, and immediately, she noticed a panicky spirit in me. She seems to have noted the changed pattern of my breathing. Elise then said,

> *"Something wrong, David, what is it? You seem to have changed your mood. The facial reflection of joy that your face had seems to have gone."*

In response to her, I said,

> *"Please make me understand. Did I take the wrong flight? Ontario, from my geography studies, is in Canada, and if I heard it correctly, we are heading to Ontario. This being the case, how will I ever get to Fuller School? Can God be so unfair?"*

In response, Elise said:

> *"David, God is never and will never be unfair. Remember what he says in his Word in Jeremiah 29: 11, that he has good plans for us. This Ontario is not the one in Canada, this one is fifty miles North of Los Angeles. In your thinking, you conclude that you have taken a fight, but God has a reason for drifting you fifty miles north of Los Angeles. You have already*

indicated to me that you are not only a Christian but a minister of the Gospel as well. Then, trust in God. You will be in very good hands with a pastor who is meeting me at the Airport. He is the coordinator of the conference I am heading to and he is meeting and welcoming people at the airport and then handing them over to others to take them to their respective hotels. He is such a fine Christian; I am sure you will be happy to meet him. He will take care of you and will make sure you get to Fuller. Just remember the Words God told Joshua, in Joshua 1: 9, 'Do not be terrified; do not be discouraged, for the Lord God will be with you wherever you go.'"

Meanwhile, I got engaged in telling Elise many things about Kenya. Elise then pulled out a book from her bag entitled 'Healing Presence' by Leanne Payne. She said,

"David, I was really happy to meet you. You have so much enriched my life, especially hearing all that God is doing in Kenya, all those Christians coming to the Lord, the receptiveness of your people to the gospel and the rapid growth of God's kingdom in your country despite the myriads of problems."

She then took out a pen and signed her name on the inner cover of the book. Having signed, she handed the book to me, saying,

"David, with all Christian love, I give you this book. Read it, it has a treasure of God's healing presence."

As she placed the book in my hands, she embraced me, and her eyes were wet with tears. It was at this very moment that the pilot announced, *"We are now heading for landing. Fasten your belts and could the crew take seats for landing?"* As the plane touched the ground, I was reading the words that Elise had put down in the book. She had written:

TO DAVID GITHII:

"David, God loves you so much. The Holy Spirit tells me that you are a great leader, and God has bestowed upon you a great responsibility to shepherd people in ALL spheres of life. As you read this book, you will be bathed in the healing light and love of our Lord Jesus. I am so glad the Lord crossed our paths! In His love, Elise. Jan 6, 1990."

As the plane drew close to being still, I was so touched by Elise. I wondered why God brought her to my life and what this flight would interpret in my life. How is it that in the first two boardings to this plane, none sat next to me? It seemed to me that God had specifically reserved this seat for Elise because he had a purpose to do that. Of all the people on the flight, Elise had to sit next to me. But then I remembered how often God had brought his angels at the time of my greatest need but also as a way to cement my life in the ministry.

I remembered the two men, charcoal burners, who had saved my life from the forest guard just at the point when I was about to collapse. I also remembered that day after my father's imprisonment and the consequent deportation from Ngong, how my mother and I had to brave the precarious journey from Ngong to Gikambura. I also recalled that night when my mother, out of anxiety and desperation for a job, had mistaken the moon's light for the dawn's light and how miraculously God made it possible for us to reach my aunt's home at Thogoto during the emergency period/curfew in colonial Kenya, a story covered in Vol 1 of this book.

As we left the plane, Elise was in front of me, and she seemed to be in deep thought. At the point of checking out, I saw Elise move towards a gentleman, hug him, and she pulled him aside. I could see her convincingly talking and putting a lot of emphasis on the person she was talking to. Then, to my surprise, the man moved quite cheerfully towards me, had his hands wide open and with a big smile, he hugged me quite warmly. I could almost feel the warmth of his heart. He said,

"I am told you are David; I now take you not as David but as a brother in Christ. You are in good hands. Take courage."

He then went back to Elise and directed her to another man who was already taking her luggage. Elise then, with tearful eyes, embraced me and said,

"Goodbye, David. If we don't meet here, we will meet in heaven. I wish you all the best in your studies."

Elise then left. That was the last time I saw her or heard from her. My prayer has always been that God would abundantly bless her and her household.

The pastor came, held my hand and led me to the hotel. As we walked, he told me to trust in God and that it was now his responsibility to see that I got to Fuller School in Pasadena at the appropriate time. In the hotel, he led me to a seat and handed me the menu, saying,

"David, choose anything that you want to eat and drink. I will pay for it."

He only ordered a cup of tea for himself. Having finished the cup of tea, he said,

"Let me make one phone call. I need to connect you with not only a good but God-fearing couple that is mission-minded as well."

So, he left me. I then started studying the menu content. I finally picked on Tilapia fish and French fries. I also asked for a glass of orange juice. By the time I was done with my food, my host had not yet come back. Meanwhile, I opened Elise's book *'Healing Presence,'* and the page I opened was page 129, where these words appear,

"Worship the Lord your God, and His blessing will be on your food and water. I will take away sickness from among you… and I will give you a full life span (Exodus 23: 25-26)."

I somehow meditated on these words that reminded me of the importance of; continuous worshiping of God and laboring in His vineyard and His blessings being even upon the things I take for granted - food and water. I remember those days in my childhood when I used to go for days without food or tea. Those days, I used to sweep the house and then spread out the rubbish to seek a grain of maize (corn) that might have fallen some days back. Many times, we depended on porridge made out of corn flour. I looked at the menu and studied all that was contained in it. It contained all the best food in the world, yet my friend had said, *"Eat anything. I will pay for it."* The words of David in Psalms 113: 7-8, 1 Samuel 2: 8, echoed in my mind, *"He raises the poor from the dust and lifts the needy from the ash heap; he seats them with princes."*

I was almost concluding that God had brought me to Canaan after spending years in the wilderness, but then somewhere at the back of my mind, I seemed to resist the thought by a voice inferring,

"No. This is only a land of opportunities, but your Canaan is in Kenya because that is where my duty calls. It is the place for my destined mission, a mission to be accomplished."

At last, the pastor came and asked me, *"How was the food?"* *"Great!"* I responded. He then went on to tell me that he had talked to a young, fine Christian couple who, as he had predicted, was more than willing to host me and even go the extra mile to see to it that I would be taken to Fuller Theological School the following day (Sunday), after the Sunday service. As we drove to this couple's home, the pastor talked highly of them;

"They are both very fine Christians, very concerned with the people in need, a mission-minded couple and people who are already excited about having you as their guest. They are very exceptional people."

He told me their names were Dan and Cheryl Thompson. The way the minister talked about them created some excitement in me, for the more he talked about their lives as Christians (though without a child), the more my heart desired to meet them.

THE CONNECTION WITH DAN AND CHERYL

At last, we were finally knocking at their door. Then, there came this short young man who offered me continuous broad smiles. He introduced himself as Dan. As he gave way, my eyes came in contact with this charming lady who was somehow taller than her husband. She shook my hands and, with a cheerful, warm, welcoming voice, said, *"David, we are happy to have you as our guest. Please come in."* Dan led me inside the house, leading me to a room and said,

> *"David, this is where you will sleep. We have made the room warm for you, and in case you need more blankets, we will be happy to give you. It's a nice room; we have placed the TV for you to watch if you so wish, but meanwhile, we can go back to the sitting room. It is important you have a bite."*

The pastor had immediately left soon after handing me over to Dan and Cheryl. In the sitting room, the Thompsons tried the best they could to make me feel at home. We chatted about the Christian life in Kenya, the political atmosphere and the way many people lived from hand to mouth. They were very much moved by the Kenyan's receptivity to the gospel. They also took a little bit of time to tell me about the American way of life, but this did not go on for long because it was already getting late, and they were concerned that I was tired. In this case, they were right. I was really tired. I then retired to the bedroom, and before long, I was soundly asleep.

I was awakened the following day around 8 a.m. I was served with very tasty food for breakfast. Then, we started the preparations to go to Church. I enjoyed the worship, which was being handled by the minister who had picked me up from the airport. After the service, the Thomsons took me around the city where they lived and exposed me to some of the American parks and other attractions in the environment. That evening we continued with our talk in regard to African ways of life and even touched on matters to do with a genuine Christian lifestyle. They also took time to encourage me in regard to my studies at Fuller. They talked highly of Fuller School saying that it was one of the best well-known theological schools in America. It was well founded on scriptures and, more so, the school of World missions.

They told me to be aggressive in my studies, and they looked forward to attending my graduation. They also assured me of their support when required and within their ability. They then explained the fact that they were to leave very early in the morning for work.

THE JOURNEY BY ROAD TO FULLER

They had organized with one of their Church members, Timothy, to pick me up at 11 a.m. and drive me to Fuller Theological Seminary. They, therefore, explained to me how I would prepare the breakfast. Cheryl said,

> *"David, while in this house, treat it as yours. Take anything you want from the refrigerator. We have stocked it with many choices of food stuff. It seems we Americans are spoilt or, should I say, greatly blessed."*

I woke up around 9 a.m., had breakfast and true to Thomson's words, and as to the custom with all Americans, Timothy came on time and before long, we were ready to leave. After I had locked the door, I kept the keys where I had been advised to leave them under the mart next to the door. As Timothy drove, I kept on enjoying the land sceneries, but I was also amazed by the many lanes in the Californian freeways. I noticed that the road we were driving on had eight lanes one way. The vehicles were so many that, they looked like a flowing river of vehicles. One could hardly cross from one side to another. I also noticed that the fast vehicles drove to the left lanes, and the slow ones drove to the right lanes. At one point, I pointed to Timothy, my amazement at what I was seeing. I said,

> *"I never saw so many vehicles and so wide roads with so fast-moving cars in Dubuque, Iowa. Also, unlike Iowa, there is no sign of much farming in California. I also note a lot of big cities, which I suppose have many industries."*

To this, Timothy responded by saying:

"David, one thing you will notice here is that life here in California is as fast as you find these vehicles moving - it is important that you prepare your mind psychologically for a very fast-moving life. You will notice a lot of take-away restaurants because people eat as they drive or even as they are involved in some activities. I am glad that you have already noticed some agricultural differences between California and Iowa. I hope that during your stay in Iowa, you learned that Iowa is situated in what we call 'Corn Belt.' It is the basket of the USA as far as corn production is concerned. In fact, California is not known for much farming; it is known much more for its industrialization, yet this state has about thirty million people, most of whom are engaged not so much in farming but in various industrial-oriented jobs. Cities like Los Angeles, San Francisco, Sandiego and others are very industrialized places. I am sure God will give you an opportunity to visit these places in the course of your stay here. If anything, California is known for fruit production."

In response, I said,

"I also notice that, unlike our country, I don't see people walking. I can rather see many vehicles but no people walking at all."

Then Timothy, with some facial expression of surprise, said,

"What do you mean, David? Does it mean you have many people walking rather than driving in your country?"

I then explained the fact that, in Kenya, my estimate of the vehicles registered by then was like 200,000, yet the population was 30 million people. This means one car for 150,000 people. While in America, 99% of the population own cars. I could see Timothy's eyes widely opened in disbelief. No wonder his next question was,

> "You mean all these people walk, and they own no vehicles? I then told him that many people walk for long distances to reach their destination."

I knew of people who would walk ten to fifteen kilometres to reach their places of work and then go back to their homes in the same way. And to add insult to injury, most of these people could not manage even lunch for they earned meager salaries, averaging $1 per day. In saying this, I was thinking of people who walk from places such as Kangemi, Kawangwere, and Kibra, among others, to the Industrial Area. They live a hand-to-mouth kind of life. As I explained all this, I could tell from Timothy's facial expressions and the tone of his voice that all that I was saying wasn't creating understandable images of this truth in his mind. The more I talked, the more distorted images formed in his mind. He then asked me, "Now tell me, David, have your parents ever owned a car?"

I then responded,

> "They had never owned a vehicle, and there was no hope of them ever driving. My father owned a bicycle, and he had to deny himself some very important things in his life in order to buy one. And by virtue of having a bicycle he was considered

as one of the able people in our community. And leave alone driving, surprisingly, I don't remember a time a vehicle ever came to our home compound."

Timothy, whom I had by now learnt that he preferred being addressed as Tim interrupted and said,
"David, I cannot trust my ears in what I am hearing from you - tell me, do you drive yourself, and if so, at what age did you get into driving?"

Then, in response, I told Tim that it was my second year since I had my first driving experience. I told him how I had to walk long distances in my ministry work trying to reach out to people and Churches. I also used public transport and, at times, a bicycle. This was the same scenario even the time I served Rongai Parish for two years, a parish that was comprised of twenty congregations.

It was the people of this Parish who, having noticed my industrious nature in the ministry and yet out of their poverty, decided to carry on fundraising to buy a vehicle for me. Through this fundraising, they managed to buy an old car registration number, KDU 386. Though this was an old vehicle, it helped a lot. I, therefore, felt happy and, at the same time, a person of a different status in life. No one owned a vehicle in our community at Mukungugu. I told Tim,
"As we speak, I have less than three years' experience in driving since the one year I spent at the University of Dubuque, Iowa, I was not driving."

Tim then posed another question,

"Now, David, putting the issue of driving and owning a vehicle aside, tell me, do you remember at what age you got in a car or bus? Many of us here in the USA would always remember the first time we got onto a plane and usually at a tender age. Of course, we have some who possibly got into a plane in the adolescence stage of their life, but sincerely, very few adult people in America have never got into a plane several times. You know, David, the more you talk, the more I feel myself a fool because my understanding is that, here in America, one cannot remember when one first got in a vehicle as all parents have vehicles, which means one is born in a home with a vehicle. Mostly, we would talk of vehicles not one vehicle. Hardly a few days pass when the child is not in a vehicle while the parents attend to various activities, including recreation, being dropped somewhere for daycare, a visit to a friend, and so on. And you know, David, here in America, 90% of young people know how to drive at the age of 18, and the majority own vehicles by that age. You will notice that at Fuller Theological School, where you are going, 99% of students drive to school. Sorry, David, for what could sound like a senseless observation, but it is because I find it hard to digest what you are telling me. This being the case, America to you must be a true representation of the biblical Canaan."

In response to Tim's observation, I said:

"It's good for you, Tim, to know that my father was imprisoned for seven years by the British Colonial Masters. At that time, I was around five years of age. I never saw him again until the *age of around twelve years. All that time, I had not set my foot in a vehicle. It was at that age that I joined standard one class (grade I) and it was not until I was in standard five that we were taken for a school tour by bus. The longest night I can remember was the night prior to going on that tour. The excitement and thoughts of being on a bus could hardly allow me to sleep comfortably. In fact, I remember dreaming a number of times being in a bus prior to the day of the tour."*

I further said,

As the sun rose in the morning, the morning would seem to drag so much. Even as our names would be called out one by one to board the bus, the time seemed to be at a standstill. The first thing I noticed as we drove off were the objects that I saw outside, which seemed to be running backwards. Another thing that excited me was the soda and the bread I had carried for lunch. This was my first experience being in a moving vehicle. That means since my childhood I had never been in a vehicle. People used to walk long distances. One could hardly see a vehicle in what we call today a location. There were very few vehicles in what we call today a County. Everything seemed to be moving backwards very fast, including trees. It took me a while to realize that it was the bus that was moving fast. There was also no one time I had ever owned a full loaf of bread. We usually had one or two slices of bread, and this was only on Christmas Day."

As I told these stories, I could easily notice that Tim was getting emotionally stressed and at times, his eyes seemed to get wet. Twice, he had wiped his face and eyes with a handkerchief.

ARRIVAL AT FULLER

We were by now getting into the city of Pasadena, where Fuller School was located and Tim made what seemed like a summary of our discussion. He said,

"David, I thank God that He has brought you into my life, for within that short time, you have so much opened the horizon of my understanding, and I realize how we Americans are spoilt and lack knowledge of what lies beyond the boundaries of our country. Thank you for pouring yourself out to me and so willingly doing so. I look forward to our being together more often in the future. As for now, this is Fuller School, let me park here and walk you to the admissions office to hand you over to them."

At the admissions office, my documents were scrutinized, and I was then referred to the housing offices. After about an hour, I was cleared. We were directed to the apartment that henceforth was to be my residence. After this, Tim hugged me, and I could feel the love that his heart had harbored for me. He then shook my hand, and with tears oozing out of his eyes, he said, *"Bye for now, David. I will see you soon."*

I was now alone in a place I knew no one, not really knowing how to get started. The question of how to get started was easily answered within the first three days at Fuller. The orientation time was not only to familiarize me with the social academic life and atmosphere of Fuller, but it also opened a spring of good friends.

Even without being told, I realized how friendly Fuller students were. Each one of them was so welcoming and warm-hearted. They made me feel at home. The professors made my worry drain because they were so welcoming both outside and inside the class. The international students' office easily turned into my source of comfort at Fuller. I was provided with many people to help me settle both inside and outside the class. Fuller Theological School became such a lovely home for me as it proved to be a pool of joy, encouragement, kindness, love and care. My only concern was the emptiness of utilities in the house.

CULTURAL SHOCK

One day, I decided to walk around and get outside the campus to see the surroundings. At a road junction, I found the traffic lights showing 'red.' I then checked on both sides of the road, and since there was no oncoming vehicle, I decided to cross the road because this is how I would do it in Kenya. I, therefore, crossed to the other side. I had just walked a few steps when I heard a police vehicle coming behind me with the siren on. I did not take notice of the vehicle. The vehicle kept blowing out the siren as it drove slowly behind me. They were even hooting, but I kept on going without any concern because I did not expect them to be after me. Just then, the vehicle was driven slightly in front of me, and the black American policeman spoke, looking at me. But I did not understand what he said because of his heavy accent. I thought he was just saying hi to me. I kept on going. I could not suspect that they would come after me - after all, I had done nothing wrong. So, I kept on walking. They tried a number of times to caution me to stop, but I kept on going. Then, they moved a bit far ahead of me and stopped the vehicle. To my surprise, I saw three policemen coming out of the vehicle. Quickly, each positioned himself, aiming the guns at me. Then one pointing the gun to me moved towards me, uttering some words that I could not comprehend because of his very deep accent. Again, the site of the guns pointed at me somehow made me realize the danger, and I abruptly stopped.

As the policeman got closer to me, I heard him say, "*Hands up! Hands up!*" Then I raised my hands up. As he even got closer, he said, "*Lie down with your face down.*" I obeyed. The next thing I felt was the policeman's hands in my pockets, and by then, the other two policemen had joined him. They were all searching my body. After realizing that I had no weapon, one of them said to me, "*Sir, why are you not stopping when we order you to do so through the siren?*"

In response I said, "*I don't understand the crime I have committed.*" The policeman, who was by now speaking slowly so that I could comprehend him, said,
> "*Why did you cross the road while the traffic lights were on red? This is treated as a crime here in America.*"

I then said,
> "*I am very new here. I come from Kenya, and I have yet to learn about the traffic rules here in America. We don't have traffic lights in Kenya. It is the police who control vehicles, especially in cities like Nairobi.*"

As soon as I answered, they heard my accent, and they immediately learnt that I was a foreigner, not even an armed black American as they had suspected.

One of them asked me, "*Why are you here?*" I replied, "*I am a student here at Fuller Theological School. I arrived just the other day, and I am an ordained Church minister.*" Then, the three shook my hand and said,

"Sir, welcome to America. Make sure you don't cross the road when the traffic lights indicate red. It is a very serious offence here in California. Wait until the lights indicate 'walk.'"

Another one said, *"Nice to meet you, sir. Have a good stay here in America."* This incident was a great lesson for me. I realized that the traffic rules were so different from the ones in Kenya. One thing I soon realized was that every road junction whether in the streets or the main roads, had traffic lights. One would hardly see police controlling traffic. I also noticed a big difference between the Kenyan policemen and the American police. I could hardly believe my ears when the police kept on addressing me as 'sir.' How can a policeman call an ordinary person sir, and even more a person like me who was not an American? That was something I could not comprehend, a policeman coming so much down to earth. I even realized more as to why I qualified to be called a foreigner because I was so foreign to the culture I was in.

Back to my apartment, I did not have much. There was a sofa set that I had to turn into a bed at night. I lacked utensils. I had to economize on the money I had. It was the one that I had to feed on and pay $400 per month towards the apartment rent. A lot of money was to be taken for books, insurance and school fees (tuition). Unless God intervened, I was very concerned that, before long, I could be experiencing acute hardships in my domestic life. I had not known that after Tim bade me farewell, he had passed through the international students' office and had gathered the information on the fact that, Fuller was not a boarding school and each student was on his/her own. One had to feed and dress, himself/herself, furnish the house, and acquire all the necessities etc. Two weeks had gone by and I was strategizing on how to get settled. I had realized that food was really dear. Utensils were also expensive and I wondered how to get going. I was somehow getting stressed.

THE VISIT BY TIM AND THOMSONS

It was around this time that I was so stressed, one Sunday afternoon, that I heard a knock on the door. Upon opening, the smiling faces that greeted me were the faces of Dan, Cheryl and Tim. It was Dan and Cheryl who had hosted me the first two nights of my arrival in California and had then requested Tim to drive me to Fuller School. Each of them embraced me so warmly. For the first time, it clicked to me that God had provided me with beautiful angels in this foreign land. Before they got in, they opened all the doors of their vehicle, including the trunk, and kept on unloading. There were all kinds of utensils one would need in a house - from knives, spoons, plates, cups, iron boxes, frying pans, cooking pots of different sizes, etc. There were also all kinds of foods, including rice, meat and much-packed food - food that would take me a good number of days. It reminded me of the way God fed people like Prophet Elijah when he was in a desperate situation and the way John the Baptist found honey that he fed on in the wilderness. They also gave me some money to keep me going. The Thompsons and Tim kept me company until very late in the afternoon. Before they left, we prayed. Then, each one of them emotionally hugged me and left. From then onwards, the Thompsons used to make arrangements for me to visit them regularly.

Each time I visited them, they would take me to a supermarket and ask me to pick anything that I needed.

When I seemed not to take as much as they wanted me to, Dan would always pick more and more of the items he suspected that I required. Since January 6th 1990, the day I first met the Thompsons, until the time of writing this book, the Thompsons have remained dear friends. They have always encouraged me to visit them any time I have an opportunity to visit America. They live in Sacramento, California. The first time I met them, they had no children, and at times, we used to pray that God would bless them with children, but the best intercession, in this case, was when my wife Lucy prayed for them in 1993 when she had come for my graduation. They believe that, that was the breakthrough. Since then, they have been blessed with four charming children: one boy and three daughters. The Thompsons were a great catalyst for my education and ministry. Their love and concern over the years have a great mark on our lives. They have never visited Kenya, but we keep on wishing that they or their children will manage to visit Kenya and bear witness to the ministry they have always cherished. Words fail me to reveal exactly that which is treasured in my heart in regard to their support. One of their children, Samuel Thompson, has been a great support in our lives.

6. ENHANCED MIRACULOUS PATH

MY ENCOUNTER WITH FLANAGAN-MIRACLE ON TUITION

Though I was getting food and clothing support from the Thompsons, I was beginning to feel some strain in buying the many books needed for my studies and the tuition. The latter was becoming a great concern. It was while my mind was getting tossed about, as far as the availability of tuition was concerned, that I went to the history class that was being handled by Professor Paul Pierson. Upon entering the class, and before he did anything else, Pierson drew my attention and said, "*David, could you see me after the class?*" Then, he continued with his lectures.

At the end of the class, I approached Pierson before he was finally done with putting together his books and notes. I said, "*Yes, Paul, you told me to see you at this time.*" Paul, getting his hands in his pocket, said, "*Yes, David, I have something that I think is yours to handle.*" He took a letter from his pocket and said, "*David, this letter is addressed to me, but treat it as your property and respond to it.*" He then shook my hand and left.

Relentless Life Bumps

Pierson had come to know me through my correspondences both from Dubuque, Iowa and Kenya. He was aware of my struggles in trying to be where I was at Fuller School. It was through him that I received the $5,000 scholarship from the Presbyterian Foundation. This had finally acted as the key to finally making it possible for me to come and pursue my studies at Fuller School. Looking at the envelope, the letter indicated that it originated from St. Andrews Presbyterian Church, Newport Beach, California. If you remember, this is the Church that I had written to in the course of my struggle to raise funds, the Church that indicated that though willing to support me (despite the fact that they didn't know me), their mission budget had been finally utilized and hence, they could not support me but promised to continue praying for me.

I had sort of forgotten them since they had not left any room for future support to the extent that, even for the short time that I had been in Fuller, I had not enquired about the whereabouts of St. Andrew's Church. When I opened the letter, I found that it had been written by Bill Flanagan, the Church Mission Chair. He was the very person who had written the response to my letter in which I had requested some financial support to help me attain the I-20 to enable me to come to Fuller. The letter, in part, said,

"If the person by the name of David Githii will ever get admitted at Fuller, please let us know. We would have some interest to partner with him in one way or another."

I then immediately rushed to my apartment and made the call to St. Andrews Reception Desk. When the phone went through, I said, *"Good afternoon. Can I speak to Rev. Dr. Bill Flanagan?"* The reply came, *"This is Bill Flanagan Speaking."* I went on, *"Oh! How are you? This is David Githii, the Kenyan Presbyterian minister speaking."* Bill then said, *"Yes, David, how is Kenya?"* I went on, *"I am not calling from Kenya. I am calling from Fuller Theological Seminary; I have been here now for the last three months."* Then Bill said,

> *"How nice to hear that you are with us, David. Now David what is the best time that I can come and we share about your life here in America and especially your academic life at Fuller school?"* I said, *"Friday is a good day. I don't have classes on Friday."*

True to his word, Flan came at the specified time. He is such a wonderful person full of love and concern, a lover of mission work. Talk of mission, and you capture his mind. We talked for more than an hour and he was all the time taking notes. Finally, he said,

> *"David, I am very happy to meet you. I am looking forward to sharing more about your ministry in Kenya and your studies here at Fuller. Meanwhile, I will share your story with our Mission Committee in which I am the chair. In the near future, we will arrange how you will come to join us in our Sunday service at St. Andrews Church. We are located at Newport Beach."*

He then left. A week later, I met someone within Fuller campus who, in his introduction, mentioned his area of residence as Newport Beach. I asked him whether he knew of St. Andrew's Church, and he told me that it was not far from his home. He added, *"Anytime you would like to visit that Church, I will be more than willing to take you there."* Upon showing him my interest in visiting St. Andrews, he took out his diary, and we set a Sunday that he was to pick me up from my apartment and drive me there.

It was a warm day when we started for St. Andrew's Church. We met Flanagan, getting ready to get into his illuminator's class. This is a class for the singles. Bill was so surprised and happy to see me there. I explained to him how it became possible for me to be able to worship there. After his class, he introduced me to the members, and he then took me to the sanctuary for the main service. I was again introduced to the congregation and the senior minister, John Huffman. After the service, a couple approached me and introduced themselves as Joan and Fred Hearn. This couple offered to come with me to St. Andrews Church any Sunday that I opted to go there. This was possible as they lived beyond Pasadena and would then stop by my apartment to pick me up. With this offer, I became a regular attendee of St. Andrews Church.

On another Sunday, I met another couple - the Brooks. They were also members of the Mission Committee. They greatly backed up the agenda of my support when it got floated in the committee. When finally, my agenda was tabled in the Mission Committee, three important results cropped out.

One, the committee passed a resolution that the Church would henceforth meet my return air tickets all the time that I would be willing to go home to be with my family. In this case, every summer, I used to go home. Two, they decided to further support me with air tickets to Scotland to enable me to carry out the research on my doctoral dissertation. Three of them also resolved to top up my tuition with $2,000 per year. This was possibly a 1/4 of the fees I was expected to pay per semester. I found a source of love at St. Andrew's. The congregation is so loving and mission-minded. This Church has the added blessing of having a dynamic senior minister, Rev. Dr. John Huffman. There is nothing else I so much enjoyed like John's sermons. His sermons captured the congregation. I found the other ministers and staff at St. Andrew's wonderful and so loving people. If it happened that my friends were not going to the Church, then the others volunteered to pick me up from my house and take me to St. Andrews Church. A person like Mcwhertor used to drive twenty miles all the way to come and pick me up. Such people also drove me back to Pasadena. St. Andrews had such loving people. To be associated with them was one of those great miracles that God was performing in my life. But there was this other miracle that I cannot forget. Even as I write, my heart misses St. Andrews Church, its wonderful congregation and its staff.

MY ENCOUNTER WITH JOHN

YET ANOTHER MIRACLE ON TRANSPORTATION

One day, I was coming from the library and heading for a bite in a small restaurant on the school campus. Somewhere midway between the library and the restaurant, I met a person who greeted me and initiated a talk. He said,

"I heard you say you are from Kenya. Which part of Kenya?"
I gave the reply, *"I hail from Kenya, a place known as Njoro, about one hundred- and twenty miles West of Nairobi."*

As we continued to share, I noticed that where we had met, there was a person already seated on a small bench. I also noticed that this man was listening eagerly to what we were saying.

Finally, we parted company with the person I was talking to. The other person seated on a bench walked towards me and said,

"Hi, sorry for acting as an intruder in your talk but I could not avoid listening to you, especially when you said you are from Kenya. I intend to go for missionary work after my studies here at Fuller which is in the next five months. My wife and I are searching for places to go for mission work and we were thinking about Kenya among other countries."

He continued;

"Unfortunately, we only know Kenya by name. I was wondering whether you would make time when you can join

us for dinner and hence have time to share with us about your country."

We then agreed on a date that I was to visit their home. After my visit to their home, they became such good friends. They made sure that I had what I needed in my house. The man sought some jobs for me. He could drive me to work and pick me up afterwards. These were jobs that I would do for a few hours per week as a way of earning an income. Then, one day, the man told me,

> *"David it is important that you get a driving license. You never know. One time, you might get a vehicle because it is not a luxury but a necessity here in California, or America, for that matter. So, do you care if I give you a few lessons per day? Of course, there will be a driving test. It sometimes happens even to Americans who come from other states."*

I responded, *"What a wonderful idea! I will greatly appreciate your support on this."*

For the next few weeks, John scooped at least an hour from his busy schedule to give me some American driving lessons. After constant lessons and assurance that I had mastered the American traffic rules and roads, he took me for the driving test and had me drive back. On the third day after I passed the test, John came to my apartment late in the evening. He told me that he would like me to take him somewhere the following day. I complied, and he made a comment on his way out of my room,

"David, God loves you, and it seems he has opened doors widely for your support. Nevertheless, it doesn't surprise me because you are one of the few people I have met who are so devoted to prayer and faithfulness. Let's see what He wants to do tomorrow."

John had been used to talking so positively about me. His words, as he left my house, didn't make me question the motive behind him saying all that. John reported to my apartment around 9 a.m. As we got in his car, he said,

"David you are a Californian driver, you have the key, so drive. Our destination is the motor vehicles department here in Pasadena."

Following his directions, we finally reached the motor vehicles department. As we left the vehicle, John told me, *"David, can I have your school ID? I want to have your correct names."* He requested that I accompany him. On getting into the office, he asked for some forms. He filled them. I was not paying any attention even when he asked me to sign one of the documents. Having waited for about forty minutes, he was handed in some documents. After this, we headed for home and he insisted that I drive.

Finally, we parked the car next to my apartment. As I went out, I handed him the vehicle keys. He looked at me with eyes that were puffed up with love towards me and said,

"David, as you can see, my wife will soon deliver our third child. In fact, we have talked with my wife, and we have found it necessary we buy another bigger vehicle as the family is

going to expand. We have already bought the car, and because you are such a dear brother to us, we have decided to give you this vehicle."

He then handed the document to me and said,
"We have given the vehicle to you with no strings attached. We have loved you naturally. We have valued your wonderful call to the ministry. Let me now walk home."

You are already a blessing to us. I remained seated in the car, wondering whether I was in dreamland. I talked to someone who parked next to my vehicle not because I wanted to talk to him but it was because I wanted to be assured that I was not dreaming.

John had always assured me that they would not come to Kenya for mission work because they had learnt from me and others that there were not many Lutheran Churches in Kenya. They were Lutherans, and their focus was Tanzania or another country I can't remember. After six months, John and his family left Fuller School with their family of three kids. They were heading for Ohio. They called me the third day after they had left Fuller to tell me that soon they would be home. That was the last day I ever heard from them. To me, they were God's angels sent to rescue me. God has many angels in our lives. It was an angel who led me to John. I now had a vehicle to take me to St. Andrews. The vehicle became my stepping stone. It was of very great help for it enhanced my mobility. The person (angel) was made to meet me exactly where John was seated on a form so that John heard that I was from Kenya and an interest to meet me was motivated in him. Thus, as the devil uses demons to attract us through people, so does God use His Spirit to support us in accordance with His purposes through people.

7. MONTE VISTA GROVE HOMES

YET ANOTHER MIRACLE ON ACCOMMODATION

While other areas of my life seemed to work, one need was pressing hard. The apartment I lived in was now becoming a bother for me to meet its rent. I was sure of meeting the cost of the next month only. Thinking about this was becoming a constant worry, and my request for support from the people I knew proved fruitless. St Andrews Church had expressed their inability to support me beyond taking me home and the top-up tuition. The money I got from my working schedule was to support my family at home and to meet some personal expenses. The Thompsons could not give me any support on this. The school was very particular when it came to payment of house rent. But even if I were to use my earnings to pay rent, they were far below the required amount. One was given a two-month grace period, failure to which one would be rendered homeless and without a house. It was almost impossible to continue with schooling. It is for this reason that I was very nervous and in an intense prayer mood.

There was a denominational program set for Thursdays. This was for the fellowship of individual denominations.

Incidentally, the student's body comprised of many denominations. Since my coming to Fuller, which was by now a duration of six months, I had never attended even a single Presbyterian fellowship. There was this day at the time of my morning devotion, that I felt an urge to go to attend the said fellowship. So, when the time came for the fellowship, I went to the notice board to check where the Presbyterians met. All the way, I knew that, that fellowship was dominated by students affiliated to PC (USA). At least 99% of them were Americans. That is why I possibly never felt as part of the fellowship. I felt like an outsider. But this time, I went to where they were gathered. There was no other black person. In their midst, I looked like a black bean in a sack of white corn (maize). They were like 200 people.

As the fellowship progressed, a time came for the newcomers to introduce themselves. When it came to my turn, I introduced myself by giving my name and the name of my denomination, the Presbyterian Church of East Africa.

Finally, the fellowship came to an end. I was quickly on my feet as I wanted to have a cup of tea before getting into the class, but then my rushing off was checked by someone. The person seated third to my left held my jacket to stop me from rushing outside.

Upon stopping, I noticed that he was holding what looked like a letter addressed to Dr. Toay, and the handwriting was mine. He asked, "*I heard you say you are David; might this be your letter?*" I scrutinized the letter and immediately recognized my handwriting. I thought it had been in my pocket and it had fallen down. Hence, I said, "*Yes, this is my letter.*" The man introduced himself as Campbell and an assistant minister to Rev. Dr. Toay at Downey Presbyterian Church. He was pursuing his theological studies. Campbell then went on to tell me that he had been given that letter a week ago by Dr. Toay, who had just received it. He (Campbell) said,

> "*Dr. Toay tells me that this letter took so long to reach him because you forgot to put a stamp, and hence it came by sea.*"

Campbell went on to tell me that Toay had instructed him to have that letter and keep an eye on the school campus and if he happened to see me (if ever I came there), to go ahead and organize how Toay could meet me. He then called Toay, informing him that he had finally found me. He told Toay,

> "*I have finally crossed paths with David from Kenya, do you have an idea on the day we could make an appointment for you to meet him?*"

Toay gave him a date, and we both marked our calendars. We scheduled the venue to be within the campus. When the assigned day of our meeting finally came, Toy arrived on the campus. Upon shaking my hand, he then warmly hugged me. He said,

> "*David, it is so nice to meet you. I remember our meeting at Dubuque in Iowa when I had come to give a lecture there. I am*

also happy to know that you finally made it to this wonderful school."

After further exchanges of welcoming words, Toay asked Campbell, *"Now, have you already identified the place in which we can have a delicious lunch for David?"*

Campbell, pointing to the nearby school café, said, *"We can feed him here."*

Toay responded immediately by saying,
"There is no way we can feed David here; we need to take him to a more executive and presentable restaurant."

He then summoned us to get into his car. After about a 15-minute drive, we came to a very modern hotel. Having sat down, Toay pointed to the menu and said, *"David, make your choice. We are here to dine with you."* Toy hardly knew that I could not differentiate nor identify with the various foods. To me, the American food was very different from what I ate back in Kenya. The menu lacked the choices of chapati, nyama choma, mukimo, karanga, Githeri, etc. It lacked ugali, mandazi and even rice cooked in an African style. To avoid much frustration, I told my friends, *"I will eat Pizza."* I had eaten pizza a number of times and I had come to like it. Toay said,
"Come on, David, there is far, much better food in this restaurant than Pizza. Why not go for another choice?"

I fumbled a bit as I tried to answer him, and I think he noticed that I was becoming uncomfortable. Campbell said,

"Pizza might be an appealing food to David. I also used to like Pizza, so let us go ahead and order food according to one's taste."

When I noticed that Toay was uncomfortable with pizza, I said, *"Okay, let me go for a Tilapia and French Fries."*

Finally, we were all settled. After we had finished eating, it was then that Toay went ahead and said,

"You know, David, your letter dated October 25th requesting support to enable you to come for further studies never reached me until a week ago. I can hardly understand why it has taken so long - almost eight months, though it came by sea. But David, sometimes God's ways of doing things are beyond our comprehension. The truth of the matter is that whatever He does, He does it with a purpose. But one thing is true: even if your letter had reached us on time, there was no way we would have come to your support."

Toay then went on to explain how small his Church is and that although my letter got to him late, it didn't make much difference because his Church could not be in a position to support me. Their Church budget was much squeezed, and they were even abandoning some long-supported mission endeavors.

After further explanation of how his Church is, he said, *"Despite all that I have said, is there anything you think I can help you with?"* In response, I directed him to my already pressing and acute concern. I said,

"*I am paying a house rent of $400 per month, and the money I had is almost finished - my worry is what to do after that? Yet Fuller administration is very particular on the timely payment of house rent.*"

After absorbing my problem, Toay went into deep thought. Finally, he looked to Campbell and said,

"*Surely, there is no way our Church can help David; they would even hate to hear anything like that. I would be nervous even to hint such a thing to them and I don't blame them. I know they are not in a position to support not only $400 but even as little as $100.*"

Toay then looked at me and said,

"*It is the way I have explained to you David; though I sympathize with the situation, I can only pray over it and hope that God would intervene. I do agree, it is a serious concern, and praying we have to pray. We will just begin here, and therefore, let us hold our hands, and I will pray for David.*"

Toay prayed a very moving prayer, thanking God for having taken care of me right from the time of conception, my childhood, my youthfulness and in my adulthood. He thanked God for making it possible for me to come to America. He prayed for my family back home and prayed that even as it seemed that I was between the Pharaoh's mighty army and the Red Sea, God would intervene and as He did through Moses when a broad way was created in the

Sea, that in the same way, a broad way would be created to help me pass through the sea of that great need. Toay had held my hand tightly in the course of the prayer, so much so that the warmth generated by that tight grip seemed to warm my heart, feeding my mind with positivity, especially when he quoted Matthew 19: 26, which says, *"With God all things are possible."*

This quotation triggered a voice in my mind that kept on whispering to me, *'He is able; He is able...'* The prayer was so touching that as we said Amen, tears were oozing out of my eyes, and so were Toay and Campbell's eyes.

As soon as the prayer was over, we left the hotel. I was taken back to the campus, and when each of them had hugged me, Toay got in the vehicle, and as he started the engine, he said to me,

"David, be assured that you will be constantly in my prayers. I will also share your predicament with intercessors in our congregation so that they will keep you in prayers, and you know prayers change things."

THE BREAKTHROUGH

Three weeks had elapsed since I was with Toay. I had totally exhausted all avenues of seeking support. As much as I tried to trust in God for the provision, my faith kept waning away so fast. But there is this morning, I had awoken in the middle of the night for intensive intercession pleading with God to send his angelic messengers with keys to open a door for support. That day, I left my apartment at around 9 a.m. for classes, and after classes, I went to do some class research assignments. This means I had not gone back to my house. I finally came back to my room around 3.30 pm. After I had been in the house for about ten minutes, the telephone rang. I picked it up and said, "*Hello.*" Then, a lady's voice from the other end said, "*Hello, David, please, let me connect you with Dr. Toay.*"

Then came the voice,

"*Hello, David, this is Dr. Toay. In fact, I had instructed my secretary to give you a call every thirty minutes since 10 a.m. Now, David, without wasting what might be very precious time, listen. I talked to Bob Lalta the director of the Monte Vista Grove Homes, where I am a member of the board, in regard to support for a place for you to stay.*"

In response, he said that he had a room but that it was already reserved for another Kenyan person who was supposed to come and occupy it this very day. And that he hardly has another house that he could offer. That was the only one available. I insisted that you are at a critical moment as you will soon be homeless and, in that connection, will be disqualified from continuing with your studies. Bob Lalta is a person who respects me greatly. The Lord helped me to convince him that he can as well give you an opportunity and guess what?

He finally said,

> *"Toay, let us put it this way: whoever of these folks comes first, it is him that I will offer the house.' Now, David, this is why we have been making all these calls to you since 10 a.m. David, do you have means by which you can get to the Monte Vista Groves Homes? It is about fifteen minutes drive from your school."*

I then said, *"Yes, you just give me the directions."* As soon as Toay gave me Bob's telephone number, including the directions, I immediately made a call to Bob's office. The secretary responded,

> *"Monte Vista Groves, can I help you?"* I said, *"My name is Rev. David Githii, a student at Fuller Theological Seminary. I have been advised by Rev. Dr. Toay to get in touch with Bob Latta."*

The secretary then said, *"Keep on hold."* Then came the voice, a very friendly voice,

> *"Hello, David, welcome to America. We are happy to have you and guess what? We have a house for you! God has made it possible through your friend, Toay. In fact, I had told him that we had tentatively reserved the house for a Kenyan person whose phone call we were expecting today and since you are*

the first to call, then the house now belongs to you. Now tell me, are you able to come now? We are eager to show you your residence for the rest of your stay at Fuller School, and David I repeat again, as long as you will be here in Pasadena, there is no hurry from our side to have you leave."

Immediately after conversing with Bob, I contacted a classmate who agreed to accompany me to Monte Vista Grove Homes. After twenty minutes, I was in the compound of Monte Vista Grove Homes. This is a very clean residence of both retired Presbyterian ministers and missionaries. After I packed the car, I proceeded to the office. At the entrance I met two ladies and a man who were chatting. They were in their 80s. They looked at me with very pleasant faces. They shook my hand, and I could feel the love and friendliness emanating from their elderly hands. They asked me,

"Are you just a visitor, or is there someone in particular you want to meet?"

I am sure they expected me to be a black American, but immediately, I responded to their question. They learnt from my accent that I was possibly from Africa. I explained that the director had asked me to come and meet him. They looked very excited. One of them asked me, *"Are you the person we heard that might come and live among us.?"* I said,

"I have come for that purpose but I understand there was another one earlier expected. Personally, I am excited that the Lord has paved the way for me to come and live with you."

Upon hearing this, they all shook my hand again and summoned four other people who were checking their emails to come and greet me. This first meeting with these folks was an eye opener that, at last, God had given me a *"Canaan."* I could immediately tell that I was in very good hands, and as life proved later, there was no other better place that I would have ever lived. This place was a good reminder of Canaan, a land flowing with milk and honey. I was then taken to the office, where the secretary welcomed me with a wonderful smile and a hug. She said,

"David, welcome to Monte Vista Grove - your source of joy. You will be loved and cared for."

Holding my hand, she led me to Bob Latta's office. Even as we opened the door, Bob was on his feet. He came towards me with his hands up in the air, giving way to his total chest to embrace me. With a big smile and a wonderful hug, he said,

"How wonderful to have you here, David. We have a place for you - both in our hearts and in our residence".

He then released me, directed me to a seat and we immersed ourselves in a lengthy discussion. He learnt about my family, my ministry, and the Kenyan life in the social, spiritual and political aspects. After this, Bob took some keys and said,

"Now David, let me show you your next residence as long as you are here in Pasadena until such a time you are done with your education."

It took us a bit of time to get to the house, as we stopped several times for introduction to all those we met, as it was the time the residents were heading for their evening meal in the cafeteria's dining hall. Each of them looked so excited that I would be living among them.

Finally, we got to my apartment to-be, 15E. It was a nice apartment - self-contained with a big sitting room, a big kitchen, wardrobes and a carpeted floor. Bob said,

"David this is not the way we want this house to look like; you are such an important person to live in a house with this kind of old carpet. In fact, this room lacks many important things. We want to make you feel loved and valued. So, what I suggest, unless you think otherwise, is for you to continue living where you are for the next week and give us some time to make this room hospitable for you. We want to have everything renewed, including the refrigerator, TV, gas cooker, bedding and utensils. We will also do some renovation."

Even as he said this, I was wondering what the house lacked. To me, it looked like the best house I had ever lived in. To start with, I had never lived in a house with a carpeted floor. The carpet they called old looked so new to me. To me, the bed was the best, the blankets, the kitchen, the bath room, name it. Nevertheless, I responded to Bob's request, *"Yes, I will be away for one week, although the house looks okay to me."*

Bob then escorted me to the parking lot where I had left my car. As I drove away, Bob said, *"David, we love you. Thank you for accepting to live in our midst."* On the way back to the campus, my friend who had accompanied me to Monte Visit Grove said,

> *"David, you are surely dearly loved by God. How I wish I could afford such a house and live in the midst of such a community! I tell you, not even five per cent of Fuller students live in such luxurious housing. In fact, ninety percent of the students lead a life of great struggle, especially when it comes to housing and school fees. I am an American citizen and we live a life of much hustling."*

I then engaged in telling him how I had seen the hand of God intervening in my life at critical times. I explained to him the struggles I got into in raising the tuition fees and how God used both Kirk Patrick, his wife and even Paul Pierson for their hand in raising the required $12,000 to enable me to have the I-20 sent to me. I also told him how St Andrews Church had come into my life and the positive contribution they were making to make my studies at Fuller materialize. My stories and experiences left him amazed at how God can be so vividly active in the life of a person he loves and has chosen to accomplish a mission. No sooner had I arrived at my apartment than Toay called me (I am sure he had talked to Bob). He could not hide the joy that had embraced him. He said,

> *"David, do you know that God loves you? Remember our prayers at the hotel. Do you know that since I left you, I have been severely on my knees, interceding for you and asking God*

to do something towards your residence? I am sure you had also prayed."

In response, I said,

"Words fail me to express my gratitude to you. God has used you mightily. I especially will never forget that prayer in the hotel, that tight warm grip you gave me as you held my hand in the course of that prayer, and the love and concern that was carved in your face and voice. Let it suffice to say, thank you so much and may the Almighty God bless you and your household mightily."

I then explained to Toay of my experience at Monte Vista Grove. The love I experienced in the hands of Bob Latta, his secretary and the members of the community that I met. Toay also talked highly of the Monte Vista Grove residents, saying they were sincere Christians, most of whom had labored in the Lord's vineyard for years. They would boldly say, like St. Paul,

"I have finished the race; I have kept the faith. Now there is in store for me the crown of righteousness which the Lord, the righteous judge, will award to me on that day" (2 Timothy 4:7-8, NIV).

This was one of the things I came to affirm when I finally settled among these people. To live with them was like living in the midst of angels. They were so loving, so concerned, and so willing to help in every way possible. They reminded me of the *'Apostolic Church community'* in Jerusalem.

FINALLY, A RESIDENCE AT MONTE VISTA GROVE HOMES

After the end of one week, I moved from my former apartment on the campus to the new campus. I was so warmly received. A potluck (get-together) was prepared as a way of welcoming me. Within one week, my apartment had been so thoroughly prepared. A new carpet was installed, a TV set was in place, there was a new gas cooker and the bathroom was renovated, among others.

In other words, it was like the old utilities had been taken away and replaced with new ones. The understanding was that I was to provide for my own meals. That is, I had to cook for myself. This was not very easy as I had to work, attend classes, and do the assignments. Thus, I also had to use the little money I got from my work to buy food and also send some to my family. I had not realized that the community had already noted the pressure I was undergoing in my daily schedule.

It was one month after my settlement when, one day, I received a call from the director, Bob Latta. When I got into his office, he said,

"David, I have further good news for you. Some of us have noticed the pressure you are facing in your daily schedules. I tabled this concern in our Board of Management, which comprises ten members and of which Dr. Toay is one of the members."

Dr. Toay spoke very convincingly about your life and the need to give you what he called, *'complete support.'* By this statement, he meant being supported in meeting all your meals and thus relieving you from cooking. In this case, he clarified,

> *"The Board of Management of this place has passed that you be taking all your meals so long as you will be a resident of this place."*

It sounded like a dream in my ears but that was the whole truth. I would no longer think of what I would eat or drink so long as I resided in Monte Vista Groves Homes. God had finally provided me with both room and boarding. I would also access all the facilities on the campus, including the washing machines. If I lacked anything, I had just to call the office and request for it.

It was while I lived there that I came to know Ralph and Eleanor Oltmans. This was an elderly couple from Minnesota who, for years, had involved themselves in volunteer services in many parts of the USA, especially in the institutions. It was on the same basis that this couple had come to reside at Monte Vista Groves for about three months. We often sat at the same table during mealtime and, especially breakfast and lunch. It was at such times that we held what we used to call the *'African stories forum.'* They were very eager to hear things related to Africa and, in particular, Kenya. Thus, I used to talk about my country and the culture in relation to the American culture, things to do with politics, education, family life and others.

We continued to be very good friends even after they went back to Minnesota. They were the main support system for my children's education, especially Amos and Nicholas, at the University of Dubuque. They would send them clothes, utensils and all sorts of items for personal use. They are also the couple who introduced me to El-Bethel Presbyterian Church in South Korea - a Church that I had continued to be in touch with for some years. Thus, from mid-1990 to mid-1993, I lived at Monte Vista Grove, and I lacked nothing in terms of room and boarding facilities. At times some of them could help me with money to send to my family for their upkeep. But beyond that, they could not cater for anything else like tuition or other academic needs.

8. TOUGH ACADEMIC TIMES

It was one year to the end of my studies when I faced quite an uphill task in my financial and academic sustainability. The previous sources of my tuition and other academic sustainability financial support dwindled with time. Some of the Churches and individuals who had supported them in the past could no longer support them. Some of the Churches had their mission budget cut by half due to the economic situation, and some had their membership decline. The strain increased as the first semester of 1992 came to an end. I already had a bad experience. I had a good friend from Zaire. In fact, we were both schoolmates at the University of Dubuque and we had both found admission at Fuller.

He had struggled to get money for the education, but having failed to raise funds to meet the payment of tuition, he was finally served with a letter giving him ten days to clear the accumulated debts, failure to which he was to be deported. Unfortunately, he never managed to get funds to clear the debts. The consequence was that he was given orders to leave the USA. It was a very heavy time for us as I helped him to do the packing. I then drove him to Los Angeles Airport. He went back home having not completed his degree course. This bitter experience was so fresh in my mind when one day, as the beginning of my final semester approached, I was served with a letter from the school office, which in part read,

"David, we have given you quite ample time to pay the accumulated school debts, and we are now giving you 10 days, failure to which you will be deported back to your country. You have also to show that you have the funds to register for the forthcoming semester. This is our final warning and communication."

As I read this letter, the memories of escorting my friend to the airport clouded my mind. Without even being told, one can imagine my emotions when I received this letter. The memories of the departure of my friend - the way I helped him pack and the way both of us were in a mournful mood as I drove him to the airport, were so fresh in my mind. The imagination of the plane taking off and looking down on the widespread Los Angeles city and the idea of terminating my studies greatly disturbed me. I embarked on calling those people who had supported me in the past, but the replies I got made my heart sink even more.

The secretaries of the Churches would say something like;

"David, I am sorry, the pastor you knew left us, and our new minister does not know you."

Another minister would say,

"I am sorry, David; we have greatly cut down our budget and we cannot be able to support you. Meanwhile, I will keep you in my prayers."

Thus, many of the people I contacted sympathized with my situation, but they were handicapped as far as supporting me was concerned. My friends in the Monte Vista Grove community had nothing to give for my problem in the current situation. The accumulated money had formed a mountain none dared to climb. The supportive St. Andrews Church had no room to accommodate this debt. More than any other time, I needed God's intervention on this problem. As I meditated, I remembered these words:

"I lift up my eyes to the hills. Where does my help come from? My help comes from the Lord, the maker of heaven and earth" *(Psalm 121: 1-2).*

There were also these words,

"Those who trust in the Lord are like Mount Zion, which cannot be shaken but endures forever. As the mountains surround Jerusalem, so the Lord surrounds his people both now and forevermore" (Psalm 25: 1-2).

Moreover, I clung to the words,

"Trust in the Lord with all your heart and lean not in your own understanding, in all your ways acknowledge him and he will make your paths straight" (Proverb 3:5-6).

Even more encouraging were the words in Philippians 4: 6-7:

"Do not be anxious about anything, but in everything by prayer and supplication with thanksgiving, let your requests be made known to God. And the peace of God, which passes all understanding, will keep your hearts and your minds in Christ Jesus."

All these biblical references seemed to open a curtain in my mind. It made me visualize that my only outlet in this problem was through prayers. In this way, that anxiety was not going to build up in my mind, causing a lot of damage to my body. In praying, I was not required to confront God in anger but rather to look back on my life and give Him thanks for what He had helped me to accomplish in the past, bearing in mind that if God had never made it possible for my father to come out of prison in 1959, I would never have acquired even primary education. More than anything else, God had bestowed upon me His grace in a manner that I had never deserved.

I then remembered those days both at Subukia and Nakuru town where my life left a lot to be desired. I even remembered those early days when my father served seven years in prison and how, in those days, I went many nights without food, had no bed, and used to sleep inside a torn sack. I remembered how I also wore a torn shirt and a pair of shorts; those were the only possessions I had. As this tape of life unrolled on my mind, I became spiritually conscious. I then felt and experienced the peace of God, which passes all understanding, embracing my mind. I settled on praying, realizing that it was the only option for my salvation.

In praying, I decided to go the extra mile. My Church had not encouraged people to kneel in prayer. The Scottish missionaries who planted Presbyterianism in Kenya never emphasized kneeling at times while praying. During my life in the Church, right from my Sunday school days, the emphasis was *"Hearty"* kneeling (Maru ma ngoro) rather than the physical knees.

This time around, I decided to pray at least three times a day, and each time to kneel physically. I folded up a woolen winter jacket that I had. I then placed it on the floor next to my bed. The first thing I did on waking up was to kneel on it and thank God for His wonderful works in me, His salvation, my calling into His Ministry, providing me with already three degrees (Bachelor of Divinity, Master of Arts in Religion and Master of Theology in Missiology), giving me a wonderful family and surrounding me with loving people both at home and in America. Each time I knelt three times daily, I had many areas surfacing in mind to offer thanksgiving for. At the end of each praying time, I called upon God not to allow me to go home without finishing my education. I remember one time, according to what is recorded in the gospel, I asked Him to give me a fish whose mouth I would open and get out the required money to meet the accumulated tuition for the new forthcoming semester.

In my persistent prayers, I reminded God of the difficult situation I found myself in when I was raising money to meet a target of $12,000 to get the I-20 and how, in His own miraculous ways, I finally made it. I reminded Him how I was stuck at Fuller when it almost became certain that I would run out of money to meet my house rent and how, in His own ways and timing, He provided me with a house at the Monte Vista Grove Homes. This was an accommodation package with an unlimited stay and provision of free meals in the course of my stay there. I even thanked Him for Churches like St. Andrews Presbyterian Church located in New Port Beach, people like Bill Flanagan, Dan and Cheryl Thompsons and their mother, Toy Mobley. There were also Churches like First Presbyterian Church - San Diego and people like Valerie and Rich King as well as David Aldridge.

Rich and David were my former classmates at the University of Dubuque Theological Seminary in Iowa. I thanked Him for some individuals from the St. Andrews Presbyterian Church in New Port Beach. Such included Fred and Joan Hearns, the Books, Mcohertor and others, not forgetting Dr. Huffman, the Church senior Minister who worked hand in hand with Bill Flanagan to see that I got some topping on my tuition from their Church, including the air ticket to fly home to be with my family.

As much as I had prayed for six days, I did not see any light at the end of the tunnel. The deadline given by the school was fast approaching. Only four days were left before the school's deadline. On the seventh day after praying, at around 11 a.m., I decided to take my car for what was not a serious oil leakage. I just decided to do so so that I could have a reason to move out of the house and at least have something to occupy my mind. Otherwise, on normal days, I would get busy with classes and beating the deadlines of assignments, and I would have hardly treated that minor oil leakage as a priority. Thus, I got in my vehicle and drove for about five blocks or a quarter of a mile to where the vehicle repair garage was.

THE MYSTERIOUS SIDE PATH WALK

The mechanic promised to give me a call as soon as the vehicle repair was over. I then walked on the side path. The traffic is flowing on my right. Upon arrival back to my house, I knelt on my usual winter jacket and, as usual, earnestly prayed that the good Lord would so miraculously open an avenue in the Red Sea. I prayed that He would pave the way for me to reach that beautiful Canaan of my academic dreamland. I prayed for the fulfillment of a wonderful ministry back in Kenya. I especially visualized my wonderful teaching in the Theological Institutions and other places of higher learning. I dreamt of my big role in contributing to the growth of the Presbyterian University of East Africa and how a good education would open my ministry to many corners of the world. I was determined to finish my education and go back home. I was totally opposed to the advice from some of my Kenyan friends who advised me that I could shift to another state and hibernate in America. The reason given is that the schools never made a follow-up on the person who had his/her education terminated. This would be so as long as the person did not claim any attachment with the institution under which one was undertaking their studies.

In such a situation, one would pursue a Green Card and, later, Citizenship. None of these appealed to me. My vision was to complete my studies and go home. I loved my family more than dollars or American citizenship. I could not wait to go back and be supportive of the lives of my kids, including their academic support. I had just finished my prayers and was enjoying a glass of apple juice when the phone rang. It was the mechanic. He said,

"Hello David, your vehicle is repaired. In fact, it was not a big deal. You just come with twenty dollars."

I sipped up the juice, and within five minutes, I was on my way to the *"vehicle's hospital"*. By now, the state of my mind had changed. For reasons best known to God, I was feeling so relaxed. Some mysterious peace had engulfed my mind. This was contrary to what one would ordinarily expect, bearing in mind that by now, there were only four days left to go. My mind should have been clogged up with worry and the fear of the unknown. My *"being"* was quite calm - my bowels were functioning normally, and I slept peacefully. I had sweet dreams the previous night. Thus, as I walked back to pick up my vehicle, I was very relaxed. In fact, I kept on enjoying the flow of the vehicles now to my left and also the buildings to the right. I was about two blocks from where my vehicle was when my eyes caught up with the name 'Africa' to a door on my right. I stopped and looked at it curiously.

The name 'Africa' in such a place would obviously attract the eyes of one from Africa; I now read the words as *"Africa Relief Enterprise."* I don't remember the exact wording, but these words were part of it. The next thing I remember is my going towards the door and rather unconsciously knocking at it. Then a lady's voice said, "*Come in.*" I opened the door slowly. Inside was a young lady who was the secretary. She greeted me with a broad smile that exposed her beautifully constructed and well-patterned teeth. She had brown hair and she looked smart and one carrying some authority. As she shook my hand, she introduced herself to me. I also introduced myself as David Githii from Kenya, East Africa. I do not remember the name of this lady, but I will call her Terry. This is how our conversation went:

Terry: *David, welcome to America. How long have you been here?*

David: *Well, I have been here for three years, being a student at Fuller Theological Seminary.*

Terry: *I hope the learning has not been rough for you especially having come from a different culture, and English being not your mother tongue.*

David: *Well, I have enjoyed my studies - by the way, would it be possible for me to say hi to the director if he/she is in?*

Terry: *David, that would be a wonderful idea, but Mr. Keith, our director has just come in. He has been away a few days, and he has instructed me not to have him interrupted because he is opening a pile of letters that has accumulated in the course of his being away - he has also, phone calls to respond to others he is calling involving our enterprise*

David: *What does your company do?*

Terry: *We deal with some relief food and charity work in Ethiopia.*

David: *That is wonderful. Ethiopia borders Kenya, but is there a way you can organize for me just to greet the director?*

Terry: *David, I have already made it clear to you that Mr. Keith is busy at the moment. If you really want to greet him, come next week, possibly on Thursday, today being Tuesday. I could tell from Terry's facial expression that she was becoming uncomfortable with my insistence that I see the director.*

David: *I do understand that he is busy, but I promise you not to stay for more than two minutes. Please treat this as a favour you are doing to one who is a foreigner and one associated with where your company operates, that is Africa. With this further persistence, Terry's face was already red with anger, and her eyes never liked me anymore. It was with that mood of anger that she quickly went, opened the director's door, and she talked to him. I now could see the director as the door was wide open. As Terry talked to him, he had his head up, and our eyes landed on one another, and he produced a wide, loving smile to me. I also offered a smile to him. The next thing I saw Terry coming back, never talking to me and settled in her chair. As she had left the door open, I now saw the director standing up from his chair and was busy, arranging two seats facing one another in front of his desk. Before long, he came smiling towards me and stretching his hand to greet me. He said,*

Keith: *"Welcome, David, as you may have been told, my name is Keith. You have done me a great favour because I have always wanted to talk to someone from Kenya. What a wonderful day."*

Keith led me to a chair, and as we chatted facing one another, our conversation went something like this:

Keith: *"Welcome to America."*

David: *"As Terry has told you, my name is Rev. David Githii, from Kenya."*

Keith: *"What part of Kenya are you from?"*

David: *"I am from Nairobi, from where I ministered in a Parish known as Loresho."*

Keith: *"What has brought you here in America?"*

David: *"I came here slightly over three years ago to pursue my theological education with which I look forward to having a wonderful ministry in my Church."*

Keith: *"What is the name of your Church, David?*

David: *"It is the Presbyterian Church of East Africa."*

Keith: *"Then you serve a Church where I have a good friend by the name of Rt. Rev. Dr George Wanjau, I am sure then you know him."*

David: *"Yes, Dr. Wanjau is not only my Moderator of General Assembly but also a good friend. In fact, he is the one who wrote a letter recommending me to Fuller Theological Seminary, highlighting the importance of my education as far as my contribution to the teaching life of the Church is concerned. He is such a spiritual man of God."*

Keith: *"That has given me a good base with your connection. Now David, tell me, how are things for you at Fuller?"*

David: *"Well, all is well. I have been making good grades and the teaching staff is so supportive. A Fuller environment is wonderful, students are very friendly and willing to share their feelings and experiences."*

Keith: *"It's good to hear that, David, sometimes we worry because many foreign students travel a rough road in their studies. Now tell me, David, do you have a family, and if* so, are they here?"

David: "Thank you for the concern. I have a family with six kids and, of course, one wife, and they are all back in Kenya."

Keith: "That is hard for you, staying so far away from your family. What are the names of your children and of course, your wife?"

David: "Their names are Benson Githii, Sammy Gichuki, Amos Ndicu, Nicholas Githang'a, Mary Wangari and Teresiah Njoki. My wife's name is Lucy Wanjiku."

Keith: "It seems you have a wonderful family, but I am sure the kids are keeping your wife busy, as well as obviously missing you. By the way, it sounds great that you are faring well in your studies and other aspects of life. Many students, including those from America, have always some struggles in their studies."

David: "Yes, I really like my family. I treat all my kids equally and my wife is such a wonderful mother and wife. Knowing that she is there for the kids and for me makes my life here at Fuller quite smooth. As for life in school, I would call it God's favour.

Keith: "David, can you tell me some of the aspects that are making the Church in Africa grow so rapidly? I am sure you have already noted how our Churches here are dwindling in numbers."

David: "There are many factors that are contributing to the rapid Church growth in Kenya is more so because there is a high degree of receptivity to the gospel. Their cultural set-up is also an advantage. This is unlike the USA, where the spirit of individualism is quite alarming. In Kenya, the spirit of individualism is quite low." I went on to say,

Materialism is a dominant factor in the USA. Again, in Kenya, people thirst for the word of God. The Churches are giving breathing space to the old arteries of mainline Church traditions, some of which are engraved in the Western culture. Some of it was mixed with the gospel that was presented to Africans by the pioneer missionaries who claimed their culture represented true Christianity."

Keith: *"David, it is good you have mentioned these things that are greatly influenced by church traditions because some of our Church leaders are so rigid with individualism and materialism, so much that they would better witness the Church dying rather than yield to a new profile of Church life. We need you people to come here and guide us into experiencing some revival."*

David: *"Coming here as missionaries would be a good thing, but you have to understand that it will not be easy to break the already established culture of materialism, individualism and the trust in technology, some of which are building into what seems to be 'cultic'. How do you get these people to listen to you being a poor person dependent on the same people for everything? Nevertheless, I don't want to renounce the power of the Holy Spirit. God is able and we have to keep our trust in Him."*

Keith: *"Has it been easy for you to go through your studies using English, which is not your mother tongue, though you speak English so well?"* I am assuming some of the professors would have a deep accent that could be tongue twisting as they speak.

David: *"I haven't experienced any problem as far as language is concerned. In addition, the professors at Fuller are very understanding and practice a lot of patience. I would say it has been fine. After all, I have done all my studies in English as it is the medium of instruction in our Kenyan schools. My studies at the University of Dubuque also acted as an eye opener."*

Keith: *"You know, it amazes me how God has been so kind to you. He is so much with you in the course of my studies at Fuller, very few people - even Americans -would have a smooth road in a four-year study period without experiencing bumpy places in the academic life."*

It was at this juncture that my mind got triggered about my present ordeal-lack of tuition, about the fact that I was somehow on my way home. It appeared like I was in a long dream in which someone had now asked for the third time whether I was experiencing any problems in the course of my studies. But I had said all is well, twice. This was now the third time Keith was congratulating me for undergoing a smooth time. But now the words *'bumpy places in the academic life'* had triggered my mind to the fact that all was not well. Then, in an emotional response, I said,

David: *"You know, Keith, for reasons I cannot explain, I have all the way forgotten to let you know the fact that unless God intervenes, I am on my way home. I feel that the Lord wants me to share with you my financial predicament , and that is why the Holy Spirit keeps urging you to* come up with a concern for my academic welfare. Right now, I am currently travelling not only on a bumpy road but on a rocky road as well."

Keith: "You can't say that David - all the way you have given me the impression of a wonderful academic life that has made me amazed. Now tell me, what is this rocky road?"

David: "I am sorry for what seems like the tactical work of the devil. He had blocked my mind, and I thank God that he has finally used you to unlock my mind. You will be surprised to hear that I will only be a Fuller School student within the forthcoming three days excluding today. I have accumulated money on tuition. I also don't have money even to register for the fourth semester. As we talk now, I have a letter in which I was given ten days' notice to clear the outstanding amounts, failure to which I will have my academics terminated, after which I am expected to leave for home. Only last semester, I escorted a friend of mine to Los Angeles Airport. He hailed from Zaire. He was also served with a letter giving him ten days as final communication to pay the money, failure to which he would go home. And since he failed to raise the money, he had his studies terminated. Now, unless God intervenes miraculously I have not many hours before I become a victim as well."

Keith: "David, this surprises me because since we started talking, you have not given me even a hint about any academic problems you are facing. But I should also tell you there is no way we can negotiate any support from our organization. We are an organization by constitution

bound not to give any help out of famine relief. We
strictly operate in Ethiopia on food relief mission. But all
said and done, I would love to see that letter. We have
people in our organization whose primary duty is to pray
over the needy cases. We have such people scattered in
the entire world. I can share your story with them."

David: "I concur with you. I am a strong believer in the power of
prayer. I have the letter in my house. I would be willing
to bring it to you within the next few minutes if you
would like to see it."

Keith: "Well, David, I would love to see that letter, it's not that I
am promising you any help, but it breaks no bone by me
having a look at your so victimizing note. What I suggest
is that, tomorrow at around 10 a.m. bring it here, and
if you don't find me, please leave it with my secretary.
Otherwise, I presently have a heap of letters to go
through, including quite a number of phone calls I have
to make to catch up. I have been away for quite some time.
In fact, I should have scolded my secretary for allowing
you to see me, but you know David, something seemingly
divine convinced me that I see you in spite of my busy
schedule. I really don't regret it; I have learnt a lot from
you, and I would love that we have other times to meet
again."

David: "Mr. Keith, I do appreciate you for sparing your time for
me, a person you don't know and, furthermore one who
did not have an appointment with you. I also discern
something divine in this encounter."

As I talked, Keith was already getting to his feet and stretching his hand to me for a final handshake.

Keith: *"Thank you so much David, in fact it's me who should thank you. As I told you right at the beginning, I have always wanted to talk to someone from Kenya, especially to one who has tasted the American culture as well. Thus, David, it's my pleasure to have shared with you."*

By now Keith was tightly shaking my hand. I could feel the warmth of his heart, and his final smile summarized it all. Keith then escorted me to his secretary's desk, and he told her,

"David is a nice person. I have enjoyed the time I have spent with him. It is good you insisted that I meet him. He will come tomorrow to bring a note that I need to see. Please welcome him. He is a man of God. Also, pray for him and tell others to do the same. He is undergoing a very trying time."

In response, the secretary said,

"In fact, it is David who persistently pressured me to let him have access to meet you. How I even yielded to that pressure is beyond my comprehension."

As I left Keith's office, I felt my heart puffed up with joy, hope and Christ's words echoed in my mind, especially where He said, *"I am with you always, even to the end of the world"* (Matthew 28: 20). From there, I proceeded to the garage where I found my car already repaired. I handed in the twenty dollars charged, and within the next five minutes, I was in my house. As I set to prepare some lunch, I felt myself unconsciously singing the hymn, 'What a friend we have in Jesus.' My eyes also set on a saying that hung on the wall of my house,

"Don't let your life slip through your fingers by living in the past or the future. Just by living your life one day at a time, you will live all the days of your life."

Next to this was another one that read,

"The Lord is my programmer. I shall not Crash. He installs the software of His Word in the hard disk of my heart; He clicks the menu of my heart with the mouse of His Spirit as I access the Network of His outflow."

Below this was Psalm 34:10. "The young lions lack and suffer hunger, but those who seek the Lord shall not lack any good thing." The rest of the day went quickly, and so was the night. Then came the morrow that Keith had talked of. The time between my waking times to 10 a.m. seemed to pass so sluggishly. At 9:40 am, I picked up the letter and by 10 a.m. I was talking to Keith's secretary.

David: "Good morning, Terry."

Terry: "Good morning, David". What a good timekeeper. You are here at exactly the time that was indicated to you. We Americans like that. Let me tell Keith that you are here. Terry soon came out and asked me to get in."

Keith: "Good morning, David?"

He was already standing up and coming out of his seat. He gave me a very warm hug and said, *"Have you brought the letter?"* Producing the letter, I said, *"Yes, here it is."* Keith read the letter, and as he read it, I could tell the pain he was feeling on his face expressed it all.

Keith*:*

"Yes, David, I agree with you. This is a very serious matter. We need some intensified and serious prayers over this matter. As you do your jogging tomorrow, just stop by around 10:30 am so that we can pray together. I will be leaving for a meeting by 10:50 am. Nevertheless, as I told you yesterday, I do not promise you any support as our policy is totally against that. However, I will share your predicament with some of our board members. You just keep on praying. I have passed the message to many other prayer warriors and intercessors."

I then went back to my house. As I walked back, I felt myself unconsciously praying deeply in my heart. I visualized myself going to school, packing the vehicle and heading to the class for studies. I kept on shunning any negative thoughts that would invade my mind. I visualized myself being in a jovial mood as I talked to the professors about my schoolwork.

When I finally got into my house, I knelt for prayer. I thanked God for providing me with the necessary school funding in the past, in accordance with his word in Philippians 4:19. I thanked Him for being so mindful of me and of my life. Again, that day and night passed quickly. Then came the following day, the ninth day.

DIVINE PROVIDENCE

At 10.25 a.m., I started off my car for Keith's office. At 10.30 am, I was in his office. Terry looked at me and gave me one of those smiles one would hardly forget in their lifetime. She rose from her seat, came and hugged me as she held my hand, leading me to Keith's room. She opened the door and said to Keith, *"Here is our friend David."*

When my eyes fell on Keith's face, I could see a mystic joy on his face. He gave me a big smile, rose from his chair, hugged me as he squeezed his chest against mine and he looked right into my face. He reached for the inner pocket of his jacket, produced an envelope, and said,

"David, there is no other trusted God like the God you serve. David, take this envelope it contains all that the school demands from you."

I got the envelope, opened it, and to my surprise, an equivalent amount to that demanded by Fuller School, including money for next semester's tuition, was all packed in a cheque leaf. As I looked at the cheque, drops of tears fell from my eyes and landed on the envelope. I then raised my eyes to look straight at Keith's face. His eyes were well-watered with tears. We held each other tightly again for a while. As Keith released himself from my chest, he said,

"David, go to school. That cheque, as indicated, meets all the dues that you owe the school."

Turning back, I looked at Terry. She was also in tears of joy. She came towards me and hugged me and said,

> *"David, truly, the God you serve has no reservation in the love he has for you. I have been with this organization for years and I have never seen anything like this. This organization has never sidestepped its policies in support of anyone. Your case is one of divine intervention."*

I was holding the keys to my vehicle, ready to move out and head for the school finance offices.

But then Keith said, *"Wait a minute, David, do you have a job? I mean, a good job."*
In response, I said,

> *"I don't have a good job. I am currently washing the classrooms of a school after it closes at 4 pm. I am also doing the same to our school's classrooms, beginning at 5 am. They are very tiring jobs and low paying."*

At this juncture, Keith called his manager and said to her,

> *"This is a fine man of God. Put him on the payroll. Anytime he has time, let him come and work here. He has no time limit so long as we are open. Give him a non-tiring job because he has schoolwork to do."*

I left immediately for school. Before long, I had my hand stretched as I handed over the cheque to the school accountant. He asked me,

> *"David, God has visited you with a miracle? I know these people, but as far as my memory can take me, I don't remember*

witnessing them paying school fees for any other person. David, God loves you, and He is proud of you."

In response, I said,
"Yes, I know He loves me so much, and to reciprocate, I have decided to live and work in His vineyard as much as He opens doors."

As I drove back to my house, the words of Psalm 118:5-8 came into my mind:
"In my distress, I prayed to the Lord, and he answered me and rescued me. He is for me. How can I be afraid? The Lord is on my side; he will help me. Let those who hate me beware. It is better to trust the Lord than to put confidence in men. It is better to take refuge in Him than in the mightiest king."

Back in my room, I knelt for the final thanksgiving prayers. I thanked God for the many black spots of my life through which He had revealed Himself. I thanked Him for creating an avenue through the Red Sea, which had stood on my academic path.

I then went for lunch. As soon as I had taken lunch, I walked back to Keith's office. This time, he wasn't in, but I left a copy of the school's payment receipt with Terry. I chatted with her for a while as I tried to strengthen her faith. The way things had worked for me made her listen to me more. She seemed to talk about the coincidence through which I got help from Keith. But I stressed to her the fact that there was nothing like coincidence with God. But rather, it was the way God had programmed things. I made her understand that, God is often working in our lives behind the scenes.

As soon as I left Terry, I reported to the manager, who took all my particulars and assigned me work to do. It involved classifying different small sizes of carvings. These were being imported from Africa particularly from Kenya. They came in big and many containers. My work was to sort out the carvings and put a certain number on each different carving in small transparent packages. These then were sent to various parts of the USA, according to the orders requested or made. Six of us worked in this department.

I was being paid $6 an hour. Since much of my school work involved writing out my dissertation, I used to write more at night and during the weekends. Hence, I spent many hours per day working. In fact, I earned so much money that, on the eve of my departure from the USA back to my Country and Ministry, I wired some money to a motor company in Japan and by the time I arrived in Kenya, a Nissan Sunny vehicle awaited me at Mombasa. This is the vehicle that greatly helped me in my ministry, especially when I became PCEA Lay Training Director.

This position meant that I moved to many places in our PCEA Church jurisdiction, organizing and facilitating various seminars, retreats and several other ways of equipping the Church leaders and the laity.

HUMILIATION BY A PROFESSOR

Fuller School was a wonderful school. It has three faculties. They include the School of Psychology, the School of Theology and the School of World Mission. I was in the School of World Mission. It bears the word 'World' because, unlike the other faculties, the students in this school come from all over the world. Otherwise, the other two schools tapped students mainly from the USA. This helped me and all others to interact with people from many cultures. It offered a better exposure to the rest of the world than the other two faculties. Both the students and faculty lecturers/professors were very accommodating and interacted well with students. Peter Wagner, Paul Pierson, Craft and others greatly loved the students. In my first year, I focused my studies on the Master of Theology in Missions degree.

It was after graduating that I embarked on the Doctor of Missiology degree. Nevertheless, for one to get registration in a Doctoral programme, one had to read six books of his/her choice from which one was to be tested. I, therefore, picked six books, read them thoroughly and then went to the office of the professor assigned the responsibility of setting the exam. I explained the fact that I had read the books whose list I presented to him. This man looked at me with a not-so-accommodating face and said,

"Are you aware that you have no time to engage yourself in a doctoral programme and be in time for graduation?"

He further went on to say,

"Doctoral studies need more time than what you have put in. My advice is that you go and do some more preparation for this kind of study and then you enroll next year. After all, and unlike many of the students we have, I understand you have no problem in the area of house rent. Why this hurry? He continued to say,

I am sure you have heard of the English saying that, 'Hurry, hurry has no blessings.'"

In response, I said,

"One thing that is pushing me urgently is because I miss my family, and I want to go home as soon as possible."

He responded;

"Okay David, I do understand, but I stand by my words that there is no way you can cover the doctoral work within the time span you are talking of. If you have that urgency to go home, you can leave the doctoral program and go home with the Master's Degree that you have already attained. Possibly, in the future, you can come for doctoral work. Otherwise, you are not an angel to achieve your present dream."

I then pleaded with him to set the exam for me because, despite the fact that I was not an angel, I still believed in the Word of God in Psalms 37 verse 4, which tells us that God does fulfil the desires of our hearts so long as we trust him and then do our part to work hard.

The professor did not speak to me again. Rather he studied the list of books I had given to him. He then asked me, "*And how is it that you did not pick any of the books I have authored?*" He was correct. I had deliberately avoided taking any of his books because I knew that he was so well-versed in the content of those books, and I thought it wise not to read any of his books. He then said,

> "*I cannot set the exam for you until you have read two of my books. It is either you go and read two of my books, or you stop pursuing your ambitious dream.*"

He then recommended two of his big and hard books that required even more time to go through. I then went to the library and borrowed the two books. It took me another two weeks after which I went back to the professor and requested him to set an exam for me. He reluctantly did it.

I did pass the exam and ambitiously plunged into the work of the doctoral program. My doctoral dissertation title read, "*The Introduction and Development of Western Education in Kenya by the Presbyterians, 1891 – 1991.*" And since much of the first sixty years of the denomination's life interacted with Scottish missionaries, much of my research would call for my visiting the archival libraries and instructions in Scotland.

It also called for the visitations of local archives, like the Kenya National Archives. In most cases, I did my research work in Scotland during summer time, after which I could proceed to Kenya where I could compile the materials even as I joined my family. St. Andrews Church met all the expenses for the travelling and the research work. At long last, the graduation day came. My wife did come for the graduation. As I matched at the podium, shaking hands with the school's president and the Dean of Studies, I looked at the teacher who had said that I was not an angel to engage in doctoral studies, and when my eyes landed on him, he looked down in shame.

Soon after my graduation, I embarked on preparations to leave for home. I finally arrived home in the month of June 1993. The Church Appointment Committee posted me to Muguga Parish, where the PCEA Pastoral Institute was located. The aim was to have me engaged in teaching some subjects there.

9. MINISTRY AT MUGUGA PARISH

Muguga parish comprised nine congregations. They included Sigona, Kahuho, Kiambaa, Nderi, Kandegw'a, Kerua, Nduma, Nguriunditu and Gacuthi. This was a big responsibility, bearing in mind that I had some added duties to teach at PCEA Pastoral Institute. I worked hard in this parish by carrying out various teachings, conducting marriages, preaching, serving Holy Communion, Elder District Home Visitations and other parochial activities. I was also the Presbytery Clerk. Among other remarkable work I did in this parish was the construction of the office block. For many years, what was referred to as the parish office was, in the real sense, the Church vestry.

After working here for two years, the Church transferred me and gave me the responsibility to be the Director of the PCEA Lay Training Department. Here, I dwelt on training and equipping disciples, but this time, having to move to various Presbyteries and Parishes conducting seminars on equipping the Church leadership. This included ministers, elders/deacons and the laity. However, the major purpose in appointing me to this department was to pave the way for me to advance teaching in Elder Districts (small Church groups/cell groups).

Having carried out this noble responsibility for one year, one day, I happened to meet a person who handed me a newspaper article that carried an advertisement calling for any interested persons to apply for a teaching position in Church History and Missions at Daystar University. He told me,

"I just decided to bring to your attention this advertisement because this is your work. It is a must that you should send an application."

In response, I said,

"There is no job meant for a person that would end up being advertised in newspapers. After all, I feel so much called into parochial work, including carrying out some teachings within my Church. That is my present call."

The man insisted by further informing me that, the said work at Daystar was also Church related and was more national. This, therefore, meant that one had a wider scope of equipping the body of Christ. It was then that I decided to send the application. Before long I received a letter inviting me for an interview.

When finally, the interview day came, I reported at Daystar. The interview began at 9 am. I was candidate number 7, and there were 7 candidates. When my turn came, I entered the room where the interviewing panel was seated. The panel took me through the interview, at the end of which the Vice Chancellor, who was also the chairman of the interviewing panel, Prof. Talitwala, with much excitement said,

> "Now, David, you are the kind of person we are looking for. You have the job now, and we would like to have you as soon as possible. When do you think you can avail yourself?

In response, I said,

> "I cannot engage in the work immediately because I have to inform and get an okay from my Church. Besides, I am also proceeding to Scotland for a four-month study on leadership."

Talitwala then said,

> "Oh! That is wonderful. We will be happy even to meet the cost of your studies in Scotland."

I then said,

> "Thank you, but that is already taken care of by the Church of Scotland. However, I will try my best to make it happen. I shall join your faculty soon after my coming back from Scotland."

Talitwala said,

> "That is a good deal. Thank you so much, David. We look forward to your being part of the Daystar community. By the way, we are placing you into the position of a Senior Lecturer on the strength of your word, so don't fail us, please."

The whole panel then stood, and each one of them gave me a very warm handshake, each one saying, *"Welcome to Daystar."*

LEADERSHIP STUDIES IN SCOTLAND

How did I find my way to Scotland? Well, it was at the time that I was a part-time lecturer at St. Paul's United Theological College. One day, while taking the ten o'clock cup of tea in the staff room, I was talking to a lecturer from Scotland. I said to him,

"I would love to take some leadership studies in Scotland if such a door would open."

In response, he said,

"That is something I can easily handle. There is this school as well as a Retreat Centre known as "Saint Ninians" located at a cliff in Scotland. I will pursue your being admitted there for some months with a full scholarship". And true to his word, it worked out.

SENIOR LECTURER AT DAYSTAR UNIVERSITY

Before leaving for my studies in Scotland. I talked to both the Moderator of the General Assembly and the Secretary-General about my having passed the interview at Daystar and their willingness to have me within their teaching staff.

They gave me the green light and prayed for me. They also said that it was an advantage to the denomination to have people in such a Christian-based institution. Thus, as soon as my studies in Scotland came to an end, the Church released me. I then joined Daystar University. I taught Contemporary Issues, Church History and Missions. I really loved this institution, and so did the University staff.

I had taught in this institution for three years when I received a letter from the Church demanding that I go back to the mainstream Church. I could not really understand why the Church had to change its mind.

I was getting a very '*fat salary*' compared to what I could get in the Church. There were many allowances including a hefty insurance cover. All travel mileage was covered by the school. House allowance and extra teaching like evening classes and holiday teaching blocks were all avenues for extra amounts of money outside the usual salary. The average monthly earnings were substantial compared to the peanut salary one got in parochial work in the parish.

I decided to go to inquire from the Secretary-General about the cause of their change of mind. Upon getting into his office, I said to him,

> *"I have come, having received a letter from your office demanding that I come back to the church. And I wondered what transpired since the church had released me."*

In his response, the Secretary-General said,

> *"It is the Business Committee that met and decided that the highly educated ministers who are serving outside the denomination be recalled back. This is because, among other things, we are hoping to start the Presbyterian University of East Africa and will need lecturers. You happen to be one of such learned people."*

Then I told him,

> *"I will go by the decision of the Business Committee, but at the same time, I am requesting that, meanwhile, I be posted to teach at St. Paul's United Theological College."*

In his response, he said,

> *"I cannot promise that your request will be taken in because such matters are dealt with by the Appointment Committee. You will get the letter of appointment."*

With that, I left him, but I did not find it fair. Even some of my close friends asked me to ignore the decision of the Business Committee.

But I decided to obey my call to serve the Church. I also upheld my ordination vow that I would do all that the Church would ask me to do. I, therefore, tendered my resignation to the vice chancellor and proceeded to full-time involvement in parochial work. To my amazement, the Appointment Committee posted me to Mathare Parish, a parish that many pastors would liken to a big punishment because it was marked by a high degree of poverty. They had ignored my request to be posted to St. Paul's United Theological College.

And so, I reported to Mathare Parish in Nairobi, Kenya, from where I was elected PCEA Moderator of the General Assembly. My other book, *"Church Transformation through Turbulence,"* covers my autobiography within the 6 years I was in the GA Office. It is a must-read book!

This book is part of the books that cover Dr. David M. Githii's autobiography. The others include;
1. Life through the Burning Bush
2. Relentless Life Bumps
3. Church Transformation Through Turbulence: Propelled Orchestration of Church.

Other books written by the author include;
1. Progressive Infiltration of Idolatry into the Universal Church and Nations: A Chronological Perspective
2. Kenya Repent or Perish
3. How to Grow a Healthy
4. Vibrant Church Through Small Church Groups
5. Tithing: Principles and Practices
6. Phases of The Church
7. Exposing and Conquering Satanic Forces over Kenya

Remarks by Githii's children on him:

1. **Nicholas muhia**

   I grew up knowing no other Hero, but my father.
   He has been a great father to us, bringing us in fear
   of God, in Christian life. He is a role model to me,
   to whom I admire many of his characteristics. He is
   a man of courage, God fearing, charismatic
   speaker, a leader, a teacher, full of wisdom, giver
   of the needy, and a man of the people. His heart is
   in the ministry, where he has served God
   truthfully.

   May God bless you father; may he give you
   strength and good health. May he give you many
   more years. May you be loved by your
   grandchildren and great grandchildren.

2. **Ben Muhia**

   Tribute by His Firstborn — Benson Githii Muhia
   They say a father is a mirror through which a son
   glimpses his future.
   If that's true, then I've been blessed to watch a lion
   walk through fire — unburned, unbowed, and
   unbought.
   Dr. David M. Githii is not just my father. He is a
   spiritual force. A reformer.
   A living sermon wrapped in courage.
   In a world drowned in noise, he dared to thunder
   truth.
   In the midst of storms, he danced with Scripture.

And me? Well, as his firstborn, I once tried to argue with him using logic —
I lost faster than Pharaoh's army in the Red Sea!
Lesson learned: never debate a man who reads Greek, Hebrew, and Revelation for fun.
I've watched him plant seeds in dry seasons — seeds that bloomed by faith alone.
Scripture says, "The righteous man walks in integrity; his children are blessed after him."
I am that blessing. I am that witness.
Dad, you didn't just write books.
You wrote legacy — into the world, and deep into our hearts.
— Benson Githii Muhia

3. **Mary muhia**

A lot can be said about my dad, but I will keep it brief. He is a giant of faith — steadfast, unwavering, and unafraid to stand alone. He has often said that he is at peace even when others oppose him, because as long as God is on his side, nothing else matters. His strength and conviction have been one greatest lessons in my life.

Dad, I am the woman I am today because of you. Your faith has been my foundation, your wisdom my guide, and your courage my inspiration. Thank you for introducing me to faith — it has shaped my life as a wife, a mother, and the very essence of who I am. I am forever grateful to you
Wangari

4. **A. Muhia**

   My father, Dr. David M. Githii, walks in integrity like few I've ever known. He doesn't just preach truth—he lives it. Transparent in his dealings, unwavering in his convictions, and unshakable in his faith, he has been a pillar in both the church and the community.

   As a former Moderator of the PCEA Church, his leadership was marked by bold decisions and servant-hearted reforms. He helped launch church partnerships, invested in people, and gave generously—not just in sermons but in substance. From establishing a secondary school to founding El Gibbor Ministries, his impact is still unfolding. "Mūndū mūnene ti ūrĩ indo, nĩ ūrĩ wendo." —A great person is not measured by possessions, but by love.

   Dad, your legacy isn't just in books or buildings—it's in people who now stand taller because you lifted them.

   —Amos Muhia